Ralph W. Harris

ACTS TODAY

SIGNS & WONDERS OF THE HOLY SPIRIT

Gospel Publishing House
Springfield, MO 65802-1894

02-0413

Acknowledgments

I would be lacking in gratitude if I did not express appreciation for the special help that has enabled me to produce this book, probably saving me months of research.

Robert Cunningham, a longtime friend and former editor of the *Pentecostal Evangel*, provided a list of articles on miracles that appeared in the publication during his tenure.

Steve Crane, a member of the Assemblies of God Headquarters staff, also provided printouts of information concerning stories of miracles that appeared in the *Pentecostal Evangel*.

I must also express my appreciation to the *Pentecostal Evangel* staff for their helpful assistance.

The counsel and encouragement of Joseph Kilpatrick, national director of publication, and David Womack, manager of the Ministry Resources Development office, have also made my work easier.

Most of all, I thank God for providing this opportunity to render a service to His people. The Vatican Museum in Rome, Italy, contains among its many treasures the largest painting ever created. In Latin at the bottom of the art piece are the words which translated mean: "Not unto us, not unto us, unto Thee be the glory." Those words express my feelings about my part in producing *Acts Today*.

Let us look forward to the last great miracle of this age, the Rapture, and the never-ending miracle of heaven.

Library of Congress Catalog Card Number 94-73270
International Standard Book Number 0-88243-413-6
Printed in the United States of America

Table of Contents

Foreword

Why would any author at the end of the twentieth century spend the time and effort to compile and document contemporary testimonies and then link them to the Book of Acts? The answer is enlightening and important.

The Book of Acts is, by and large, a record of testimonies. It gives irrefutable witness to the power of the Spirit in the lives of real people who face the timeless struggle between the religion of form and force, theory and reality, faith and works, and the constant war between principalities and powers.

Christianity must have Acts today or slide into an ineffective tradition resulting in dead and dying churches. In spite of all the religion in our world, the reality of broken lives and broken homes should cause every believer deep concern.

Ralph W. Harris has done the true church of Jesus Christ a great service by approaching the subject of the supernatural as he has in *Acts Today*. He has avoided the trap of creating a hunger in the reader for a revival of twentieth-century Pentecost. To the contrary, the reader will experience a growing hunger for the supernatural dynamics of a revival of first-century Pentecost. He uses the effectual manifestations of the Spirit to make us hungry for the Spirit himself.

As a church leader, I have become deeply concerned about the spiritual condition of our generation. I have lived through over fifty years of "todays," and I have seen nearly everything tried to meet the needs of each of those "todays." I bear witness to the fact that what we need in this "today" is a genuine extension of what took place in the Upper Room.

Yes, the revival we need today must begin in the individual. The Book of Acts opens with people who had come in contact with a living Christ. What separated them from others was not their experience of knowing Christ but of moving on to obey the command of Christ, "Tarry until . . ." Because of their faith and obedience, the Holy Spirit came as promised, resulting in the most powerful Church in recorded history.

And if we are to experience Acts today, we will not settle for anything less than a personal Pentecost.

A personal Pentecost opens the door to infinite demonstrations of the Spirit for the purpose of bringing into the world through the believer the ministry of Jesus Christ—in all of its supernatural power. To say "Acts today" is to say "Jesus today." The work and ministry of the Holy Spirit makes possible the work and ministry of Christ. The conclusion is clear: If we want Jesus today, we must have Acts today.

The Holy Spirit could not have chosen a better person to write this book. I have known Ralph W. Harris for close to forty years. He is an outstanding Christian. Although he began his ministry in the pastorate, early on he was recognized for journalistic as well as leadership skills and invited to the national office of the Assemblies of God; in 1954 he became editor-in-chief of the Church School Literature Department, shaping curricula and developing new pedagogical techniques until retiring in 1976. A writer as well as an editor, copies of his booklet for new Christians, *Now What?*, has surpassed the ten million mark, including numerous foreign language editions. He was executive editor for the *Complete Biblical Library,* New Testament, until its completion in 1991.

He is a man with a strong doctrinal and theological background. He has been a faithful student of the Word of God for well over fifty years. His commitment to Pentecostal, evangelical truth is unquestionable. This foundation brings great strength to his writing. You can trust him with the subject of the supernatural for many reasons: He is first and foremost a man of integrity; these testimonies have been carefully researched—you could not pay Ralph W. Harris enough money to embellish or sensationalize the work of the Spirit; above all, Ralph W. Harris is a man who has lived the life of Christ and experienced the supernatural throughout his ministry. Pentecost to him is more than a theory—it is a reality. It is not difficult to commend this book to you because it is a joy to recommend the author. I believe you will be thrilled by the testimonies you are about to read, but more than that, I join with the author in praying you will now experience Acts today.

—CHARLES T. CRABTREE
*Assistant General Superintendent
of the Assemblies of God*

Preface

Why have a book on miracles?

Because the Pentecostals, a sizable segment of Protestantism, believe that miracles are possible in these days.

Since its beginnings less than a century ago, the Pentecostal revival has swept around the world. It has become a dominant force in Protestantism and has multiplied-thousands of followers in the Roman Catholic ranks. In addition, many believers in mainline denominations have received the Pentecostal experience even though they have remained in their own churches.

From its beginnings, the revival has based its beliefs on the premise that the miracles which God performed in the first century of the Christian era can still occur. Pentecostals reject the claims of some that "the day of miracles is past" and believe that the events of the Book of Acts can be duplicated in our present time.

While we value and appreciate the work of the medical profession and know its expertise can slow the progress of disease, there come times when it reaches the end of its resources; then God does what is impossible. This book contains numerous doctors' testimonies of such supernatural intervention.

Pentecostals believe the Bible is a unique book verbally inspired by the Holy Spirit. Because of this, the Bible's records are true, and its promises are dependable.

We believe that the postsalvation experience that empowered Christians in the first century, the baptism in the Holy Spirit, is not only available today but greatly needed to provide an effective witness for Christ.

We believe that the outpouring of the Holy Spirit on the Day of Pentecost, as recorded in the second chapter of Acts, is a pattern for this experience. For this reason we believe the initial, physical evidence of the baptism in the Holy Spirit will be, as on the Day of Pentecost, speaking in other tongues as the Holy Spirit gives the utterance.

I have been a Pentecostal, specifically Assemblies of God (which has become the largest of the Pentecostal bodies in America), since my earliest days. My mother began attending Pentecostal services just before my birth in 1912, about eighteen months before the Assemblies of God was formed, in April 1914. Of my more than fifty-five years of ministry, thirty-five were spent in various positions at the international headquarters in Springfield, Missouri.

This has brought me the great privilege of associating with the Movement's leaders and enjoying a varied ministry in America and foreign lands. I have written numerous books and many articles for headquarters publications.

About twenty years ago I prepared a small book, *Spoken by the Spirit*. It was written to refute the claim by a well-known evangelical leader that there were "few, if any, documented instances of people speaking in other tongues in a known language." It was not difficult to find and record seventy-five instances, in sixty languages, of xenoglossolalia, speaking in a known language by a person who did not know it. Persons present who knew the language provided documentation.

In a sense *Acts Today* is a sequel, for it deals with other equally well-documented accounts of miraculous events. (However, because the first book is out of print, I have included some of its entries in the section on xenoglossolalia.)

I know of numerous miraculous events that could be added to those found in *Acts Today*. For example, I remember the healing of a Mrs. Carmody, a member of my home church, Berea Tabernacle, in Detroit, Michigan, when I was just a child.

While boarding a street car, she slipped and scratched her leg on the metal step. A streptococcic infection developed, which eventually became life threatening. Her husband had already made funeral arrangements when she asked Pastor J. R. Kline to let her receive the Lord's Supper. He brought the elements, and as she partook of them, God healed her completely. She lived for many years thereafter.

In 1950, when I was pastoring in Seattle, Washington, a neighbor, Carol Mittun, was planning a birthday party for my young daughter Sharon. Carol was not a member of my church, but her two little girls attended our Sunday school, and sometimes she came to a service.

I phoned her about the plans, and her first words were "I can't talk, my eye has been injured."

"What has happened?" I asked.

She answered that her three-year-old had had some scissors in her hand, and in Carol's trying to get them from her, a point had pierced Carol's eye. "I can't see," she said.

"Let me pray for you now, over the phone," I said. After finishing, to encourage her I told her the Lord would touch her.

"He already has! I can see!" she exclaimed.

Mrs. Mittun said it was like the clearing of a TV screen. The next Sunday she came to our church and told about the healing. A tiny scar could be seen where the scissor's point had entered, but she had perfect vision.

About the same time, an elderly member of my congregation, Thomas Thorsen, had an even more remarkable deliverance. As a small boy in Norway, sixty-five years earlier, his shoelaces on his ice skates had become frozen. While he was using something sharp to loosen the laces, it slipped, puncturing an eye so drastically that the fluid ran out and blindness followed.

In his seventies, Thorsen attended a Sunday afternoon healing service at another church and was healed in answer to prayer. Many people of our church could attest to the miracle.

On several occasions God has worked in a miraculous way in my own life.

In June 1914, when I was twenty-one months old, I wandered out to the alley behind our house in Detroit, Michigan. A young boy came down the alley in a light delivery wagon, pulled by a blind horse. The boy did not see me as I strayed out to the center of the alley. Miraculously, I was not trampled by the horse, but two wheels ran over me.

When I was brought into the house and my frantic mother tried to get me to stand, I cried and could not do so.

Since my mother had come into contact with Pentecostal people who believed in healing, she hurriedly phoned several friends and asked them to pray.

She then put me to bed, where I slept for a couple of hours. When I awakened, I was free from pain, and there was no evidence of injury.

As I grew up, my health was good and my life generally accident free, so I never had to spend any time in a hospital (I was even born at home) until the summer of 1967.

First, on July 29 I entered the hospital because of a sacroiliac strain that kept getting worse. I spent ten days in traction, then returned home.

The day after returning home, as I was doing some exercises my doctor had prescribed, I suffered a convulsion, became unconscious, and was rushed back to the hospital. At suppertime I had another seizure.

For the next couple of weeks I went through numerous tests that convinced the Springfield doctors I had a brain tumor. When it seemed apparent I would need surgery, it was decided to fly me to the Medical Center in Kansas City where a renowned surgeon, Doctor Williamson, specialized in brain surgery.

On Friday, August 25, I received a pneumoencephalogram test, which would show within two centimeters if a foreign object was present. The night before, the ten thousand people present at our biennial General Council meeting in Long Beach, California, stood and prayed for me. Many people and churches had already prayed a great deal; some had prayer chains interceding around the clock.

After the excruciating two-hour test, Dr. Williamson came to my hospital room that afternoon and gave me the glad news that there was no trace of the brain tumor indicated by earlier tests.

Searching for a cause of the problem, the doctors surmised it might have been viral encephalitis. This is brain fever that has its own very frightening implications. Whichever it was, God healed me. The symptoms never returned.

In late 1967 and early 1968 I was severely afflicted with arthritis, which affected my arms, hands, and torso. I needed help to put on my shoes. It was difficult to push open a car door from the inside. For five months, except for four nights, I had to sit up five or six hours nightly because numbness and pain prevented my lying down.

On March 28, 1968, I was to leave for St. Louis to participate in a Sunday school seminar for several days. This concerned me, for I would be sharing a motel room with a member of my department, and I disliked the thought of disturbing his sleep by sitting up. The National Committee on Advance, of which I was a member, was in session, and I asked them to pray that God would heal me. Beginning that night the affliction disappeared.

Is it any wonder that I believe in miracles?

Introduction

The Purpose of Miracles

What is the value and purpose of miracles?

1. Certainly, it is not to bring praise to people. If they should be involved, they are merely agents.

2. Miracles are not just to gratify God (He is not like human beings, who need to have their ego satisfied). God sees miracles as a means of furthering His great purposes, to bring people to salvation and to advance His kingdom.

The Book of Acts provides its own explanation. After the crippled man at the Beautiful Gate was healed (Acts 3), Acts 4:4 states the result: "Many of them which heard the word believed." After judgment fell on Ananias and Sapphira because of their dishonesty, Acts 5:14 reports, "Believers were the more added to the Lord, multitudes both of men and women." Acts 9:35 relates that after a man named Aeneas was healed of paralysis because of Peter's prayer, "All that dwelt at Lydda and Sharon saw him, and turned to the Lord." In the same chapter, after Dorcas was raised from the dead at Joppa, verse 42 says, "Many believed in the Lord."

3. Miracles bring glory to God. (The Greek word for "glory" is *doxa*. It means "bring honor.") In relation to God, "glory" refers to His reputation, His majesty. Miracles bring glory to God by proving His existence. Miracles cause people to revere God. The power that comes with the baptism in the Holy Spirit is given not just to perform miracles but to glorify Christ. In Acts 1:8 He said, "Ye shall be witnesses unto me" (not just "about me"). Healings reveal His power, His love, and His concern for the afflicted.

4. Miracles should increase believers' faith. This is a major purpose of *Acts Today*: to remind readers of what has happened

in the past and encourage them to believe for the present, especially youth and new converts. Some may not have personally witnessed a miracle or even heard of one.

Miracles in the Book of Acts

The Book of Acts is full of miracles. They were a major reason for the rapid growth of the first-century church.

In his sermon on the Day of Pentecost, Peter stated that Jesus was "approved . . . by miracles and wonders and signs" (Acts 2:22). In his commentary on this verse, Bible scholar Stanley Horton points out that these are "the three words in the Bible for supernatural works": (1) *Dunamis* ("power," "might") is the word used for "miracles" here. (2) *Teras* ("portent," "omen," "wonder"), translated "wonders," is always used with (3) *Semeion* ("sign," "signal").

The *Complete Biblical Library* states that "in the language of logic and reasoning a semeion is a 'proof,' something which could probably be regarded as certain." It is the word used in Mark 16:17, "These signs shall follow them that believe."

Acts 4:30 tells of the disciples' prayer "that signs and wonders may be done." Acts 5:12 reports, "Many signs and wonders [were] wrought." Stephen "did great wonders and miracles" (6:8). "Miracles and signs" were done at Samaria (8:13). "Signs and wonders" were done in the ministry of Paul at Iconium (14:3). In their report to the Jerusalem leaders (15:12), Paul and Barnabas told of "miracles and wonders God had wrought."

Questions about Miracles

Some questions about miracles no one can answer. Why doesn't God heal everyone? Why doesn't He heal people every time? Why does He sometimes heal sinners who don't repent? We do not profess to know all the answers. Faith is necessary, but it is not the only factor. Certainly, we must acknowledge and trust the sovereignty of God. As with many other questions in life, we must wait until the day when we know as we are known.

Verification

Proper validation is very important in a book of this nature. I have employed several criteria to offset possible questioning by skeptics.

Those in charge at the world-famous Roman Catholic shrine at

Lourdes, France, are to be commended for their procedures when checking on those who claim to have been cured there. The book *Strange & Miraculous Cures,* published in 1969 by Ace Books, Inc., reported the work of the Lourdes Medical Bureau. It examines all visitors who claim to have been healed. A member of the Bureau was quoted as saying, "Although there have been millions of people to visit Lourdes, we have accredited a scant 54 miraculous healings in the past 110 years. An even smaller number of these cures have been acknowledged by the Church."

I too have endeavored to be careful in validation. Otherwise I would be unfaithful to my purpose.

1. Usually I have insisted that the healings be immediate answers to prayer, rather than being gradual in nature, although I acknowledge some healings occur over a period of time. I want to refute claims that the healings resulted from the natural healing powers of the human body.

2. I have listed miracles of such a nature that skeptics cannot attribute them to coincidence.

3. I have used numerous stories from the *Pentecostal Evangel*, which uses some excellent safeguards: They check with pastors of the people involved; they usually wait three years before publishing a healing in order to confirm the cure was permanent.

4. I have asked for the name, address, and phone number of a contributor's pastor and of two witnesses. This has enabled follow-up checking.

5. In some cases my personal knowledge of contributors, people of high character, has been sufficient. I have been obliged to do this when no one else was present, as in the case of visions or angelic appearances.

However, even then there has been additional verification. In the case of visions, the results have proved their reality. In the reports of angelic visitations, it seemed circumstances were such that no other explanation would be reasonable.

Divisions

The stories have been listed in major categories, for example, Healings, Special Miracles, Xenoglossolalia.

The last division carries the title "Unusual Experiences." Here I have placed "Angels," "Demons," "Divine Guidance," and "Visions." Some may wonder why I have separate divisions for healings and miracles. While all healings are supernatural, in some instances, other miraculous aspects are present, such as faith, visions, or prophecy. In such cases these have been placed in the "Special Miracles" division.

Special Note: I have been very concerned about properly documenting the stories that appear in *Acts Today* and have carefully tried to check their authenticity. As far as I could ascertain, they are all true accounts. If any should prove otherwise, it will not be because I have failed to do my best.

Section One

Healings

All of them were healed.—Acts 5:16

The Bible is replete with accounts of the healing power of God. Soon after Israel left Egypt, God told them, "I am the Lord that healeth thee" (Exodus 15:26), and many times the Old Testament record reveals how He fulfilled that promise.

When the Son of God came to earth, healing was a major feature of His earthly ministry. In His sermon on the Day of Pentecost, Peter said of Him that He was "approved of God among you by miracles and wonders and signs, which God did by him in the midst of you" (Acts 2:22). And during his sermon at Cornelius's house, the apostle told the Gentiles that Jesus "went about doing good, and healing all that were oppressed of the devil" (10:38).

Twice in Acts men crippled from birth were healed: through Peter's ministry at the Beautiful Gate (3:1–8) and during Paul's ministry at Lystra (14:8–10).

During Philip's ministry at Samaria, many who were paralyzed and lame were healed (8:7).

A man named Aeneas had been bedfast for eight years with paralysis. He was healed when Peter prayed for him (9:33–34).

At Malta, after escaping shipwreck, Paul prayed for the father of Publius, "the chief man of the island," and he was healed (28:7–8).

In providing stories about healings in *Acts Today*, I have tried to avoid using those which could be attributed to coincidence or to the healing powers of the human body. Doctors can often stop the progress of disease, but the healing proceeds by the natural powers inherent in our bodies.

You will find here an impressive variety of healings, some of ailments judged incurable by medical science.

14

"My Healing Was Complete"

In February 1991 Mary Cummings of Shreveport, Louisiana, began to experience severe swelling in her left knee. For the next three months doctors tried various remedies, such as drainage, cortisone treatments, athletic bandages, observation, tests. Despite the tests returning negative, her knee was still swollen and hurting. She was using crutches to keep from putting pressure on it.

Finally, surgery was scheduled for mid-May; however, it too failed to solve the problem. Seven months passed, but relief did not come. Mary was getting discouraged. She had been in the prayer line so many times, she was getting embarrassed; the relief seemed to be coming in such small stages. She had found it necessary to curtail her activities in church ministries. The pain kept her from standing any longer than twenty minutes at a time.

Against her better judgment, in October 1992 Mary joined a group on a missions trip to Mexico. Although she believed God had impressed her to go, after a few hours on the bus, her knee was hurting so much she wondered if she had made a mistake. The door-to-door visitation and crusade meetings would require much standing.

After arriving in Mexico, the crusade team had to stop beside the road because one of the buses needed some mechanical work. Only Mary remained inside—her knee hurt too much to be on her feet—and lay down in a seat. She was battling doubt about why she had come.

The next thing she knew, she was awakened by hearing someone say, "Get up, it's time to go!" A half hour had passed.

As Mary sat up, she felt different and enveloped by a beautiful sense of God's presence. The pressure on her mind had vanished, and she had a sense of awe.

Suddenly Mary realized—without any kind of testing—she was healed! The pain was gone. "I had no doubt my healing was complete." For the next week she was involved in all the ministry of the team and stood for hours each day. She says, "I believe I received my healing because I obeyed the Lord."

When Mary Cummings returned home, she faced more than four thousand dollars in medical bills. But God worked in a special way to have them paid in full.

15

Cured of the Incurable

Jane Shoults is a busy person. At the time of this writing her husband was superintendent of the Northern Missouri District for the Assemblies of God, and she was Women's Ministries director. So the physical problem that began in late 1991 not only caused her extreme pain but also greatly hampered her work for God.

Several rounds of antibiotics did not help a continuing bladder infection. Then tests by a urologist showed the problem was not an infection but rather an incurable disease of the bladder lining called interstitial cystitis. A second opinion from another specialist confirmed the diagnosis.

The prognosis was that acid in foods she ate was burning holes in the bladder. It would result in scar tissue, eventually shrinking the bladder so much it would have to be removed.

The U.S. Department of Health and Human Services in Washington, D.C., further confirmed the deadliness of the disease. Some doctors consider it worse than cancer because it's incurable.

Despite a special diet, the intense pain continued. Nevertheless, Mrs. Shoults determined to carry out a project the women of the district had adopted: raising money to construct a church at Arecibo, Puerto Rico. While she was praying in December 1991, God gave her the assurance He would heal her while on the island.

A further complication arose in January 1992 when a routine mammogram revealed a malignant tumor. It required a radical mastectomy on January 24. During the operation, God performed a work of grace, giving her great peace. After surgery she needed only one dose of medication to relieve the pain and within three days was able to drive her car and shop for the trip. Two weeks after the surgery she left by plane for Puerto Rico and suffered no ill effects.

However, God was not finished. After Mrs. Shoults spoke in the morning service of the convention, the national leaders prayed for the healing of the interstitial cystitis. She had no physical sensation, but God gave her the assurance she had been healed.

Although she had been following a very restrictive diet, after the prayer session she began eating normally, with no painful results, and continued eating normally thereafter. The symptoms had disappeared instantly. I talked to her by phone in early 1994, and she was still healed.

No More Glasses

When Lillian Overstreet was eighteen months old, an injury from a fall greatly damaged her optic system, causing her right eye to slide under the eyelid until only the white part of the eye could be seen. When she was three, the doctors at the famous Wills Hospital in Philadelphia could offer no hope for a cure and could only recommend the use of glasses with strong lenses.

Within three weeks after Lillian entered public school at age six, teachers determined she could not compete with normal children. Back at the Wills Hospital, the chief surgeon stated that only immediate surgery would keep her from becoming totally blind. After a month in the hospital following surgery, the bandages were removed, and she could see—not well and not without glasses, but at least she was not blind.

The years that followed brought added problems. When she was twelve, the right eye became noticeably crooked. The left eye also was affected, causing split focus, and it began moving downward.

By the time Lillian was sixteen, the right eye was completely out of focus, and it was evident she would never have the use of that eye again. She reported, "The heavy magnifying lens for my left eye was my dearest friend." Without it she had to be led about like a blind person.

About this time, Lillian made a complete surrender of her life to God, determining to go "all out" for Him. She began a Sunday school class for kids she gathered from off the streets.

To secure training for Christian service, Lillian began studies at Eastern Bible Institute (now Valley Forge Christian College). She reveled in the Word and became active in ministry, but the fear of becoming totally blind was always present.

In February 1947, during Lillian's second year at the school, there came a time of prayer and revival. It lasted eight days, and classes were suspended. On day six the entire student body spent the morning in prayer. After lunch Lillian walked into the entrance of the administration building, one wing of which was used as a ladies dormitory.

As she started down the hallway, Lillian heard two girls praying in their room and stopped to listen. A couple of other girls joined her. Sitting on a stairway in the hall, they began to sing a hymn. The girls in the room came out and joined in the singing.

It started a "parade" of spiritually hungry students, first the girls, then fellows from another wing. The teachers heard and also came, joining in spontaneous worship. Finally, about 165 people were present.

God's presence was so near, Lillian felt she could almost touch Him. She says, "Suddenly I was overcome by the idea my eyes should be healed." A young lady who sang with Lillian in a trio gently tapped her on her elbow. They talked about God's presence and were reminded of the man who prayed to Jesus, "Lord, help my unbelief." Lillian felt impressed to offer the same prayer, oblivious to the presence of others.

Filled with faith from God, Lillian took off her glasses, and cried out, "The Lord will give me my sight today!" The Holy Spirit reminded her of John 16:23, "Whatsoever ye shall ask the Father in my name, he will give it you."

The word *whatsoever* gripped her. Weeping and quoting the promise, Lillian moved toward a familiar voice belonging to one of the many persons who were praying for her.

The young lady was praying audibly but softly, and Lillian was standing face to face with her. Looking heavenward, Lillian exclaimed, "My Heavenly Father, I thank Thee for healing me, and I accept it now in Jesus' name."

She waited. Then the young woman cried out. She had seen the eyes slip into place. She began to shout, "It's a miracle! I've seen a miracle!"

Lillian says, "I turned my head. Instantly every object, every feature, every fine line—to the end of the hallway—came into perfect focus. The misty, impenetrable veil was forever lifted."

Lillian Overstreet went on to have a Holy Spirit anointed ministry with her husband, Robert Watters. She never wore glasses again. When the doctors who had pronounced her eyes incurable tested them again, they found them normal.

Lillian Watters went to be with the Lord several years ago and is now enjoying the thrill of seeing her Great Physician face-to-face.

The Worst Case He'd Ever Seen

Five medical doctors said that Mildred Larson could not survive. For ten hours she had had no blood pressure or pulse. The situation appeared hopeless. But God healed her.

Sunday, October 10, 1954, had begun so well. She and her coworker, Linda Stiver, had come to Minneapolis for a short rest before returning to the evangelistic field. They planned also to attend Richard Vinyard's Twin-Cities campaign.

It was a great day, meeting old friends, chatting with acquaintances, and helping in the prayer room at the campaign. At bedtime Mildred felt tired and thought she might be getting the flu. She didn't realize what was at work in her body.

During the night she felt sharp pains in her head, and the next afternoon, about three o'clock, she began breaking out with red spots like measles. The doctor who responded to her call thought it might have been something she had eaten the previous night and, despite the high fever, said it wasn't serious. Friends went to get the prescribed medicine, and a prayer request was sent to the campaign headquarters.

The next thing she remembered was awaking in a hospital and learning that many hours had passed. When her friends had returned with the medicine, they had thought she was sleeping and didn't try to wake her. Later when they finally did try, they couldn't; she was in a coma.

By the time the ambulance got Mildred to the Swedish Hospital, she was also paralyzed. The doctors' diagnosis was spinal meningitis, and the prognosis gave no hope of recovery. At best, she would be left paralyzed and mentally impaired because of the intense fever.

Her body was swollen, there were large sores on her legs and arms, and the blood vessels on the sores were broken. She was bleeding internally and vomiting blood—"the worst case [of spinal meningitis] my doctor had ever seen," wrote Mildred.

When she came out of the coma, however, her mind was alert, and she was not paralyzed. But hope was short-lived, for on the second night at the hospital, the doctor who checked her found that she had had no blood pressure or pulse for ten hours. In addition, her veins had collapsed, and she suffered from terrible pains in her head and neck.

Five doctors worked on her, using long needles containing fluid to restore her blood pressure. Finally, four of them left, saying nothing more could be done. The remaining doctor advised the nurse to call a minister; Mildred would not last until morning.

Pastor John Strand came and prayed. "As he prayed," said

19

Mildred, "the glory of the Lord filled the room." An hour later another pastor, Grant Graan, came bringing an anointed cloth. Mildred placed it on her stomach and reported that as soon as she did so "the vomiting stopped." She said that the sense of God's presence, which had settled on her after the two pastors had prayed, lingered with her for days, causing nurses and doctors to marvel at her peace and calm.

During the night, the fever broke, and when the doctor examined her the next morning, he said something marvelous had taken place. All her organs had stopped bleeding, and some that had stopped functioning properly were now normal.

Eleven days later Mildred Larson was dismissed from the hospital and ministered as an evangelist for many years.

Nothing's Too Hard for God

July 1970 was a dark time for Vernon Pettenger and his family. His physical condition had forced him after nineteen years of missionary work in South Africa to sell everything and return home, expecting never to return. As soon as he arrived in America, he was placed in a hospital. His condition resulted from the long-term side effects of a medicine prescribed for him when it was new.

In 1954, while on the field in Africa, he had developed a skin allergy: Itchiness and sores spread until they covered his entire body. Prescribed medicines did not help, and the condition became so bad Vernon could hardly stand the touch of his clothing.

Then a doctor came by and said, "Try this, it's something new from the United States." The medication was cortisone. It worked! In a week's time his skin was normal! However, if he neglected the treatment, his skin would begin to break out again. Unfortunately, he did not know of the harmful side effects of cortisone. Ten years later, one showed up during furlough: He developed cataracts on one eye, eventually losing its sight.

Another bad side effect was kidney stone attacks. One occurred in October 1968. He expected to stay in the hospital about a week, but it took nearly seven weeks and five surgeries before he was able to go home. He learned later that cortisone kept him from healing quickly. His skin had become very thin, "like wet tissue paper." The slightest bump would tear it, requiring weeks and months to heal.

Since the density of his bone structure was only 50 percent of normal, his bones broke easily. In one year he had five major breaks. Merely lifting a heavy object could break a bone. Vernon's muscles began to weaken, making it difficult to continue the ministry in South Africa. Finally, he decided to give up, and in July 1970 the Pettengers returned home to Springfield, Missouri, to seek medical help.

However, the situation became increasingly bleak, even though a prominent doctor in the city did his best. Finally, after five months of tests and treatments, he looked his patient straight in the eye and said, "Vernon, I'm backed up against a wall. I can't do anything for you."

Vernon went to the famous Mayo Clinic. Their report echoed the Springfield diagnosis. So his doctor said, "I'm going to send you to the Barnes Hospital in St. Louis. They have the best of doctors."

Admitted to the hospital on January 25, 1971, Vernon Pettenger was sent to a room on the eighth floor. As he bent over to loosen his shoes, despair struck like a dagger to his heart. He thought, *This is the end of the road. I've come here to die.*

But right on the heels of that thought, the Lord's response to Jeremiah's doubt about his carrying on business as usual flashed into Vernon's mind, "Is there any thing too hard for me?" (Jeremiah 32:27). As these words rang in his mind, all the promises of God seemed to flow into his being. He could feel the prayers of his family and friends. God's healing power surged through him. He felt God had touched him that morning.

Shortly, five doctors walked in, talked with him a little while, then said there was little hope. The adrenal gland produces cortisone naturally, and he had been overdosing for sixteen years. They doubted the gland could ever resume its normal function. They were taking away all medication, and it could be fatal. They said they would observe his reaction, and left.

Vernon still felt overshadowed by the presence of God, and their diagnosis had not disturbed his faith.

The change was remarkable. On the third day he realized he had no rash or itching; his skin was normal. After five days the doctors came to check Vernon again. They looked puzzled and could not explain the phenomenon. They agreed to release him if he would immediately report anything unusual. He might go into a coma anytime, they said.

It was time to witness, Vernon felt, and he told them that thousands of people in America and South Africa had been praying for him, and God had answered their prayers.

As time went on, new strength came into the missionary's muscles. There was no bruising from bumps. He could carry his luggage again. After fourteen months his doctor gave him a complete medical clearance, and the Pettengers prepared to return to South Africa.

Vernon's Springfield doctor came to the Pettengers' last service before their return to the field and heard Vernon testify of his healing. Afterward he asked, "Doctor, did I say it right?"

He replied, "Vernon, more than right. God has done something very wonderful for you."

The doctor in South Africa who had attended Vernon was amazed to see him so well without cortisone. He called in his associates and nurses and said, "See this man; he should be dead." He prepared a written statement confirming that Vernon Pettenger's "past deficiencies and illnesses are only memories and scars. This can only be a miracle."

God gave the Pettengers twenty more years of effective service in South Africa.

From Blindness to Witness

Evangelist Gene Martin has made constructing churches in foreign countries an important part of his ministry. His seventy-ninth project was for a suburb of San Salvador, El Salvador, in 1975, working with missionary John Bueno (now a field director for Latin America). The brand-new church for Caterse de Julio was to be built debt free.

After the main structure had been finished, the desire of the people to lay a special tile floor themselves delayed the project. So it was decided to have services out of doors in a large open area adjacent to the new church, and they put up a few lights and began.

The first night or so a few hundred came. Then the evangelist announced that on a certain night they would be praying for the sick and that Jesus, the Great Physician, often healed by miracles without medicine.

That night a blind woman, well-known in the barrio, was brought, led by a young girl about ten years old. They joined the prayer line and finally stood before Martin, Bueno, and some elders. They anointed her and prayed a simple, brief prayer. Immediately the woman began leaping and shouting (in Spanish), "I can see! Glory to God! Thank You, Lord, my Savior!" Many others joined her in praise.

The next night, as John Bueno and Gene Martin drove toward the place of meeting, the trails were so packed with people they had to park some distance away and walk to the church. Such great throngs filled the area that to avoid the crush, many had climbed into nearby trees or onto the roof of the new church.

The missionary went among the crowd to inquire what had brought them and learned that the former blind woman had put on her own advertising campaign. She had gone throughout the barrio and urged people to come to the meeting, saying, "You can get any new part you need."

Many came and, best of all, received a new heart for the old, sinful one. Miracles are not an end in themselves but serve to draw people to Christ and salvation. The incident proved what Jesus once said, "These signs [advertising] shall follow them that believe" (Mark 16:17).

"Miracle Boy"

The doctors of Rochester, Minnesota, gently told the parents of sixteen-year-old Herbie Hoover Kinsman that he could not live. His badly damaged liver was even protruding into his chest. And he had lapsed into a coma. Hope faded for his parents, Mrs. and Mrs. Kenneth Kinsman of Iron River, Michigan. They had thought his problem was the flu, but now they learned it was serum hepatitis.

Local doctors had sent Herbie to the state's largest medical center, then he was flown to Rochester, Minnesota. The verdict there was the same. Even a liver transplant was impossible.

The teenager's family continued to pray, even after doctors warned that Herbie, who was now in stage four, a deathlike state, would die. Herbie had been in intensive care for eight days and was expected to die that night. It was Friday evening, September 5, 1975. The family now asked God for a miracle.

On Saturday morning a doctor was to formally pronounce

Herbie dead. To the doctor's amazement, the boy was still alive, but more than that, his liver was normal! At four-thirty Sunday afternoon, Herbie opened his eyes and recognized his family for the first time in a week.

Nurses at Rochester referred to the intensive care room where Herbie had been confined as "the miracle room." In less than three weeks he was able to go home. Because of the liver illness his skin had turned a yellowish-green, and the whites of his eyes were yellow. Doctors said it would be three months before his skin resumed its usual color and six months for the eyes. But the natural color of both returned in only two months.

He had lost much weight while in the hospital but gained it all back. And within three months of his release from the hospital, he had grown four inches.

Four months later Herbie returned to Rochester for a checkup. Doctors reported his liver function had returned to normal.

It is no wonder that when he returned to his high school class, the students referred to Herbie as the "miracle boy."

"A Higher Power!"

At first, in April 1948, Wildon and Florence Colbaugh thought their eight-year-old daughter, Carol, had contracted the measles like other children at her Springfield, Missouri, school. But after three days her condition rapidly deteriorated. She became increasingly distressed and vomited violently. Her temperature soared, and before her parents realized it, she became dehydrated.

At first the doctor could not determine the cause of Carol's condition. Intravenous feeding and efforts to reduce her temperature failed. Convulsions continued, and the dehydration increased. Her little body became stiff and almost lifeless.

The doctor called several hospitals in the city to find a room where oxygen could be administered, but they did not want to admit her because of the possibility of a contagion. Finally, after much persuasion, a room was made available, and to save time, the doctor himself raced to the hospital with the nearly lifeless child.

An oxygen tent was draped over Carol's stiff, emaciated body, and the parents knelt by it and prayed earnestly. The doctor offered little encouragement, only that if she lived past midnight, there would be a slim chance of survival. Later, a nurse told them that the admittance records at the hospital had listed Carol's condition as "terminal."

In addition, the chances of full recovery were small. The high fever had already affected her brain tissue, and postinfectious encephalitis had put her into a coma. The doctor gave Wildon and Florence the gloomy prediction that if she lived, she might be mentally retarded or so seriously paralyzed that she would be unable to walk, talk, or take care of herself. This was usual for patients in Carol's condition.

That Sunday night the doctor acknowledged he had done all that was possible and that only a Higher Power could bring Carol through. Loved ones stood by. At times the light of life flickered and seemed about to go out.

But while the doctor rested in a nearby room and nurses tip-toed quietly by in the corridor, the Great Physician bent low over the still form and breathed divine life into it.

When morning came, Carol was still alive. She remained in a coma for two weeks, feeding was intravenous, and great care was needed to sustain the feeble spark of life. But then she came out of the coma and was able to go home. Within two more weeks she was up and normal again.

In about a month from the time Carol had left school, she was back attending classes and was as active and alert as before. She grew up to be a healthy young woman and a talented musician. There was never any trace of the dire consequences the doctor had projected. She survived a terrible car wreck (in which her first husband was killed) and served for over seventeen years as a missionary to Senegal.

What was the reason for Carol's quick and full recovery? The exclamation of the doctor who attended her reveals the answer, "Only a Higher Power could do this!"

Jesus Kept His Promise

The doctor at the hospital in Santo Andre, Brazil, said, "One young man is beyond help; the others we are working with and hope to save."

Missionary-evangelist Bernhard Johnson and Pastor Lee Paino looked at each other in dismay. The four young men being examined were part of a group of twenty-nine young people from

California, Oregon, Idaho, and Washington. They had come to spend July 1971 witnessing and distributing gospel literature from door-to-door during the day and singing and testifying in the mass meetings at night. Many were finding Christ as Savior, and everyone was excited at being a part of what God was doing.

But now four of them, Mel Wilson, Jon Coleman, Bob Geary, and Drew Argue, were not feeling well; earlier they had asked to stay behind instead of going to the Saturday night service. The leaders suggested they remain with the group and attend the rally.

The young men had become increasingly uncomfortable, however, and by the time of the altar call, pain and discomfort were compelling them to leave the stadium and go back to their quarters.

By the time they had boarded their small bus, two of them complained of severe headaches, Mel was suffering from severe stomach cramps, and Drew had passed out. When they reached their living quarters, all four were desperately ill. The symptoms were unconsciousness, numbness, lack of heartbeat or pulse, difficulty in breathing, and convulsions.

Fortunately, they were able to get the assistance of a police officer, who rode with them to the hospital. By the time they reached the emergency room of the hospital, Drew was unable to breathe. Beth Johnson, the missionary's daughter, helped by solving the language barrier and giving mouth-to-mouth resuscitation.

Bernhard Johnson and Lee Paino were summoned to the hospital, where they heard the frightening news that one of the young men, Drew Argue, was already "beyond help."

The emergency demanded prompt action. As the two men entered the room, they saw Drew's lifeless form and Jim Boehner praying and desperately working with him. Joining him in prayer, missionary Johnson cried out, claiming the authority of the name of Jesus, calling for healing and resurrection power.

As they looked down on Drew, his expression began to change, his eyes opened for a moment, and he raised one hand to signal he was all right.

Going to the next room, Johnson and Paino prayed for the other three young men. Again God answered in minutes. So complete was their healing that within an hour all four had recovered enough to leave the hospital, and within a few days they were well and strong and able to complete their mission in Brazil.

It is believed that the four had contracted a rare form of food poisoning from tomato paste—fatal in 90 percent of the cases in Brazil. But Jesus had promised His followers that when they went out to minister in His name and happened to take "any deadly thing, it [would] not hurt them" (Mark 16:18). He had kept His word!

Expected to Die

Even before their baby girl Vickie was a year old, Mr. and Mrs. H. L. Chadwick of Levelland, Texas, realized she had a serious medical problem. When they laid her down, she could not move by herself. Even by the time she reached fifteen months, she had never been able to stand alone.

Worst of all, her head was growing larger and larger and was completely out of proportion to the rest of her body. On the back of her head a solid knot stretched from ear to ear.

The Chadwicks' doctor suggested they take Vickie to the cerebral palsy clinic in Lubbock, telling them before they left, "Above all, be sure that they examine the baby's head."

The parents' worst fears became reality that dark day in July 1952. The doctors at the clinic declared there was nothing they could do for Vickie and gave her only six months to live.

But God used a neighbor to bring hope to the Chadwicks. She told the mother that evangelist Morris Lefkowitz was conducting services at the Assembly of God in Levelland, and there was to be a special healing service to pray for the sick. Mrs. Chadwick had never attended this church before but decided to take Vickie to the meeting. What was there to lose?

Pastor Kenneth Barney reported that he noticed the child when they came into the auditorium; even from the platform he could tell the baby's head was abnormally large. When the mother brought Vickie to be prayed for, she wept as she told the pastor and the evangelist of the doctors' dreadful verdict a few days before—that the child had only six months to live. She had them feel the large knot on the back of the child's head.

Pastor Barney reported, "I'm sure every saved person in the building was praying when we laid hands on little Vickie. Seldom have I felt such a sudden burst of divine power as came into that auditorium. One of our ladies sitting in her car outside the church with one of her children testified later that she felt the power of God even out there."

A parade of divine miracles began.

A few minutes after returning to her seat, Mrs. Chadwick raised her hand to indicate she wanted to say something. With a heavenly glow on her face she announced to the congregation that the knot on the back of Vickie's head had disappeared! You can imagine how the people praised the Lord.

In a few more minutes, up went the happy mother's hand again. This time she told the congregation that Vickie had stood alone at the seat for the first time in her life! Mrs. Chadwick was almost beside herself with joy—and so was everyone else.

Vickie had never said a word except "da-da" until her healing, but the next night as they neared the church, the little girl said "church." Before long, when someone would ask her who she loved, she would say, "Jesus." Within three weeks she was walking. Her head gradually shrank to a normal size.

In January 1953 Vickie's mother phoned the church and said to the Sunday school superintendent, who answered the phone, "Yesterday was the day my baby was supposed to die, and I just wanted to tell Pastor Barney that she's the healthiest, most active child you ever saw!"

The next year Mrs. Chadwick took Vickie to the Lubbock clinic to show her to the doctor who had said she would not live more than six months. He did not even recognize her. When the mother told him what had happened, he said, "Well, I don't understand it, but I know where to take my tough cases now."

Normal Vision Restored

One Saturday morning in May 1993, Doris Brown awoke to a startling and terrifying discovery. Her vision was blurred, and when she went outside to work among her beloved flowers, she was seeing four of each blossom. Later that day she went to her optometrist for help. After examining her, all he could do to alleviate the problem was to cover one lens of her glasses with tape. But that gave her no help. In fact, driving home was doubly difficult because now she was emotionally upset.

She and her husband, Kenneth Brown, pastor of The People's Church in Arnold, Missouri, were perplexed about what to do next. They went to an ophthalmologist, whose examination cost several hundred dollars. But he gave them no clues as to what the exact problem might be.

A neurosurgeon referred Doris to the Ophthalmology Department of the well-known Barnes Hospital in St. Louis. After extensive testing, their diagnosis was that evidently she had suffered a stroke on the stem of her brain. There was no medicine, they said, which could help, and there was no treatment which could bring a cure.

It was a trying time for the Browns, who were extremely busy in the work of the Lord. Doris's vision would range from normal to double, triple, and sometimes quadruple vision. She was annoyed by the patch she had to wear, she was afraid to drive, and she was unable to perform her usual duties.

It was decided to ask the church congregation to seek God for the healing of their pastor's wife. A date and time were set, and the people were encouraged to fast and pray. The Browns asked a pastor known for faith in God's ability to heal, Tom Canter, to come.

Sixty or seventy persons joined their hearts together in faith that night of June 7, 1993. There had been fasting and prayer. And God did not fail them. Doris Brown was instantly healed. At the time this book was being prepared, the healing had stood the test of time.

Healed of Rheumatic Fever

For three days Cheryl, five-year-old daughter of evangelists Paul and Myrtle Hild, had been in a coma at a Marinette, Wisconsin, hospital. Stricken with rheumatic fever, she had been there five weeks, and now a crisis had been reached. The nurse told the parents that the 4:00 A.M. hour was approaching, a time when patients usually take a turn for the better or worse.

Even today rheumatic fever is a deadly affliction, but in April 1957 it was even worse. It caused more chronic disability in children than any other disease and was the second most likely disease to be fatal in the five-to-nineteen age-group, taking thousands of lives each year.

When the family had set out for meetings in Marinette, the parents had thought Cheryl was suffering some aftereffects of the flu, and it did not appear serious. But by the time they reached their destination, she was in much pain, and walked with difficulty, dragging one leg.

Other strange symptoms appeared: large red blotches on her legs and a swelling on her forehead. The Hilds knew their child was very sick and placed her in the hospital, where she was given tests and placed under observation.

The tests showed she had acute rheumatic fever, with a heart murmur and other symptoms. At that time in medical history it usually proved fatal. To complicate the problem, she also had a severe case of nephritis (inflammation of the kidneys) and could keep only a little nourishment in her stomach. Her body and face were so badly swollen that her eyes were almost shut, besides being very sore and sensitive to light.

The doctor's prognosis was as discouraging as her condition. "You must prepare yourself for a long vigil. It may take from six months to a year of bed rest for her to convalesce. She has an injured heart, and there will be a permanent scar."

It was Thursday, Cheryl's fifth week in the hospital, when the crisis hit like a raging storm. The youngster began to react, speaking incoherently, then went into a convulsion that rocked the bed.

Some of the nurses who hurried to Cheryl's bedside thought it was the end. The child's heart raced fiercely, she had a high temperature, and her pulse soared to 170.

Paul had gone to another state for an engagement but rushed to Marinette by plane after hearing of his daughter's condition.

After Paul arrived, the doctor checked Cheryl again, then took the parents aside and told them she was in the last stages of a coma and that her kidneys had ceased to function. All that was left was prayer and hope. Cheryl was a pitiful sight with tubes for various purposes jutting out from different parts of her little body.

The Hilds enlisted prayer help. Ministers were in conference in both Wisconsin and Minnesota, and phone calls were made asking for their prayer support. The local church also interceded.

Then came the crisis hour, and the nurse reported Cheryl was breathing more easily. By Sunday she was coming out of the coma, beginning to drink liquids, and her appetite had returned. Soon the parents were leaving the hospital, not with empty arms and heavy hearts, but with their daughter in their arms and great joy in their hearts.

After returning to their home in Minneapolis, the Hilds took

Cheryl to their family physician. The electrocardiogram showed her heart was perfectly normal, and the nephritis soon cleared up.

That was many years ago. There was never a trace of heart ailment or other chronic disability since.

Clinically Depressed—Certifiably Delivered

In early 1950 it seemed to Hildreth Ethridge (now Brissey, and retired) that she had reached the end of the road called hope. For many months she had waged a losing battle against depression of the deepest kind, fighting the attacks of Satan. Physicians, psychiatrists, and hospital personnel had done their best but without results. From their point of view the only possible help was brain surgery, even then chances of success were slim.

The problem had been developing over a long period. The young woman had become an evangelist at an early age, and God had blessed her ministry. But sad events, even when she was a child, foreshadowed a dark future: the loss of her father when she was a preschooler, a stepfather's loss of sight, the need to support herself and the family at the age of thirteen, the loss of both of her brothers only three months apart during World War II. These were contributing factors to her descent into the dark valley of mental collapse. The climactic time of illness was to draw itself out for ten months.

The audiences Hildreth blessed did not know the fearful struggles within her mind. Besides the family history, years of strenuous work, worry, and a general feeling of insecurity caused her severe mental illness.

Taking advantage of her exhaustion, Satan began his attack on her mind and then proceeded to her body. Hildreth was gripped by constant anxieties and doubts. Fear of sickness such as cancer and other diseases plagued her. Headaches and stomach trouble were her constant companions. Living up to his name as the accuser, Satan (see Revelation 12:10) tortured her with accusations and horrible condemnation, making her question her relationship with God. Although the Bible teaches that believers do not become demon possessed, it is true that Christians can become demon oppressed.

Hildreth's severe headaches kept her from concentrating in prayer. She was so weak physically that she was not able to do battle spiritually and soon lost all sense of God's presence. She continued to deteriorate after she returned home to Tulsa from the East Coast in 1949, and it was decided Hildreth needed to enter the hospital. She endured a series of electrical shock treatments but did not improve. She felt like she was on fire and pleaded for water, but drink as much as she might, it gave no relief. Demonic powers attacked her each day in the late afternoon. For weeks she had little sleep. She became like a dead person.

After a temporary release, she returned to the hospital for a new series of treatments under one of Tulsa's most competent physicians. He gave her insulin shock therapy with as much as four hundred units of insulin poured into her body at a time.

Finally, the doctor told Hildreth's mother, "There is nothing left to do except perform prefrontal lobotomy." It would be expensive, yet he hedged on its effectiveness: "There is no guarantee she will ever be normal again, but it will bring her some relief."

Mrs. Ethridge believed God's promise that He would heal her daughter, so she rejected the brain operation. Displeased, the psychiatrists told her, "You have a very sick girl. If she ever gets well, it will be a miracle."

God was getting ready to do just that. In May 1950 Hildreth was taken to another hospital for an additional series of electrical shock treatments. She had lost all sense of hope. She lay in her bed without eating or talking, not even dressing herself or bothering to comb her hair or brush her teeth.

On June 6, 1950, Hildreth received another treatment. This time it caused her to go into a coma. She does not know how long it lasted, but it was God's hour for her deliverance. Suddenly she began to pray, "My Jesus, my Jesus, my Jesus." Then she spoke the words, "I can't!" No human might could defeat the power that was opposing her. It was going to take a miracle, and God was about to perform it.

When she said, "I can't," the Holy Spirit began to pray through her in other tongues. It alarmed the doctors and nurses, and they began to give her injections to bring her out of the coma. They thought she was having an adverse secondary reaction and returned her to her room.

After recovering from the sedatives that had been given to her, Hildreth felt life coming back into her body. It was like the sensation after one's limb has gone to sleep and then begins to feel the normal circulation of blood again.

The next day Hildreth was a changed person. She felt as though she had come out of prison. There was a sparkle in her eye and a smile on her face. Her fears and anxieties had vanished. She was hungry for the first time since her ordeal began and ate everything on her plate. She got out of bed, cleaned up, dressed, and combed her hair.

At noon the nurse told her she could go to the dining hall. She asked God's blessing on the food for the first time in ten months and ate two trays of food. Then she walked to a piano that was in the dining room and began to play and sing some gospel melodies, "What a Friend We Have in Jesus," "Leaning on the Everlasting Arms," "Lily of the Valley."

When the psychiatrist heard the music and singing, he and some of the nurses left the doctors' dining room and came to see which patient was providing the concert. Later, one of the nurses told Hildreth that the doctor literally jumped for joy, clapped his hands, and exclaimed, "There's the real girl." He realized she was a normal human being again.

The psychiatrists conducted a conference about her case. They were amazed at her calm as she came in for an interview. Her doctor said, "Your recovery is marvelous. It is marvelous, indeed!" At their request she stayed two more weeks, which gave her numerous opportunities to witness and pray for other patients who came to her. Her sense of victory remained, and she continued a fruitful ministry for many years.

Broken Body Made Whole

The day had begun so well for Chaplain Talmadge McNabb that September 1966 morning in South Korea. He was to travel in a jeep with a convoy headed for a fifty-mile trip over the mountains. The panorama of shadowed and sunlit mountains under blue skies brought thanksgiving in his heart to the God he served.

This awe-inspiring journey, however, was abruptly cut short. A Korean taxi rounded a curve on the wrong side of the narrow road. The chaplain's driver panicked, swerved sharply, and the jeep careened over the mountainside into a rocky creek. The driver was thrown clear, but McNabb was pinned beneath the jeep. The driver, apparently in shock, repeatedly tried to raise the jeep, succeeding only in dropping it back down on the chaplain each time.

A truckload of Korean soldiers happened by, rushed down, and lifted the jeep. Excruciating pains made Chaplain McNabb feel as though sharp knives were being thrust through his chest. It was difficult to breathe.

U.S. soldiers radioed the command post, which sent a helicopter to rescue McNabb, but it had difficulty locating a landing site and ultimately landed some distance up the mountainside. (More than an hour had passed since the accident.) A trip by litter to the helicopter was extremely painful.

By the time the chaplain had been transported to the evacuation hospital and the chest surgeon had reached him, he had turned blue from lack of oxygen. The surgeon quickly did a tracheotomy and attached a respirator to aid his breathing. X rays showed his ribs were broken in sixteen places, and his chest was crushed.

The night before the convoy began its journey, Chaplain McNabb had written his wife: "My life is in God's hands. We never know what tomorrow holds, but we know the One who holds tomorrow." Now was the time to prove that trust in God.

After three days under the heavy respirator, Chaplain McNabb was getting depressed, worrying about his family. He cried out in desperation, "Lord, here is my broken body. You made it and have kept it in good shape through these years. Now, if it be Thy will, hear me. Please make me whole again."

At that moment something wonderful happened. It was as though the living Christ came in person and touched him. He felt the healing touch as new strength surged through his body.

That same day the chest surgeon removed the respirator, and McNabb was able to breathe normally with no pain. He asked, "May I sit up?" and the doctor agreed. Then he asked if he could try walking. To the surprise of the doctors and nurses he got out of bed, walked up the hall a ways, and then kept on. He even went to the Red Cross lounge and played the piano.

When the doctor came to his room a few days later, he said, "You must have had help from the Man upstairs." McNabb agreed. After a few days he was back on duty. When he returned to the hospital later for a checkup and new X rays, the healing had been so perfect that the doctor had difficulty identifying which ribs had been injured!

Car Demolished, Driver "A Miracle"

Bob Lundstrom, an evangelist and instructor at Zion Bible Institute, Barrington, Rhode Island, was telling his class how marvelously God had protected him in his travels of over a million miles in about forty countries of the world. Little did he know what would happen two days later, November 3, 1991. But God knew and used the event to show His power.

After classes, Bob drove to South Portland, Maine, for weekend revival services with Pastor Calvin Rogers at Cape Shore Assembly of God. After the Sunday evening service, he sat in his car and bowed his head to pray over his return trip, as he had done hundreds of times over the years.

The next thing he knew he was in an ambulance headed for the Maine Medical Center in Portland. A truck had smashed into the driver's side of his car, knocking him unconscious, pinning him behind the steering wheel, and leaving him badly bleeding. The impact had been so great that it had demolished his car and had thrown the two people in the truck onto the road.

Pastor Rogers came upon the accident scene shortly afterwards and later told Lundstrom, "There is no human way you should have come out of that car alive. This is a miracle of God!"

Lundstrom's side was badly bruised, but after several X rays, medical center personnel said he had sustained no serious injury; so he flew home to Newark, Delaware.

However, during the next weeks he suffered intense pain, and finally he went to the Wilmington, Delaware, Medical Center. Again X rays were taken. The night before he was to return to Zion Bible Institute, he received a phone call from the doctor who had examined him. "You should be admitted to the hospital immediately," he exclaimed. The X rays showed he had a collapsed lung.

Concerned about his students because he had already missed over two weeks of classes, Lundstrom felt he should return to the classroom regardless of his physical condition. However, he promised the doctor that if the pain and difficult breathing continued, he would go to a local Rhode Island hospital.

The problems did continue. Lundstrom knew that if he did not receive healing, he would be forced to go to the hospital. Through Dean Patrick Gallagher he sent word to the college's president, Benjamin Crandall, that he wanted to be anointed and prayed for in chapel the next day in accordance with James 5:14–15.

"Somehow," testifies Bob Lundstrom, "the blessed Holy Spirit helped me to put my complete trust in Jesus as my divine Healer. As President Crandall anointed me, with faculty and students gathered around in prayer, the supernatural power of Jesus Christ surged over me from the crown of my head to the soles of my feet! I was completely, miraculously healed! The pain left immediately, and I could breathe normally. That night I slept on my left side for the first time since the accident."

A week later, Lundstrom went back to the Wilmington, Delaware, Medical Clinic for more X rays. Standing beside him as they examined the results was an agnostic doctor. Amazed, he pointed to the lung that had been collapsed and was now perfect. When Bob Lundstrom told the doctor of the prayer in the chapel service, he responded, "Reverend, put me on your prayer list."

Two years later Lundstrom could report that he had preached for 115 Sundays in a row, taught ten classes a week, conducted many revival crusades, and traveled in Poland the year before.

No Cure for Leukemia?

John H. Bostrom, 66, was shocked when the doctor came into his hospital room with a report on his condition. "We don't need to take any more tests, no more examinations. Now we know what it is—lymphocytic leukemia." The minister's blood count when he entered the hospital was 770,000 (normal is 5,000 to 10,000). His hemoglobin count was 5.9 grams (normal is 14 to 15).

Bostrom, a well-known evangelist, had been serving as interim pastor at Bethel Temple in Los Angeles in February 1966 when he began to feel very tired. He found it difficult to climb the steps to the church office. It was only with a great deal of effort that he could carry on his preaching ministry and fulfill the many other responsibilities of a pastor's life.

One of his daughters noticed his extreme weariness and urged him to see a doctor and have an examination to determine what was wrong. At first he refused because he had not been in the habit of going to doctors. Later, because of her persistence and because of increasing fatigue, he acquiesced.

After the examination on a Tuesday morning, the doctor wanted him to enter the hospital that afternoon. But conscious of his responsibilities, Bostrom said no but promised to enter the hospital after the evening service the next Sunday. That led to the doctor's distressing announcement of his having leukemia.

Bostrom was in the hospital for two months. At first his condition deteriorated. He had to have thirteen pints of blood, which led to transfusion fever—producing a temperature of 108 degrees. He had baseball-size swellings in his armpits, an enlarged spleen, pleurisy with fluid in his right lung, anal and back muscle spasms, and a bowel obstruction. Once, he went into anaphylactic shock, his temperature again reaching 108 degrees.

At times his family wondered if he would survive, but one thing made the difference: They and many of the people who knew of his ministry all over the world prayed for him. When he went home after the two-month stay in the hospital, his white blood count was normal, and in a few weeks his hemoglobin was normal too. The night before Bostrom went home, the doctor came to his room with the latest laboratory report and exclaimed, "This is unbelievable." The patient told him it was because of the prayers of God's people.

Four years later when John Bostrom went for a checkup, his doctor, holding Bostrom's current lab report in his hand, reminded him, "You know, I suppose there is no medical cure for leukemia." The former patient had maintained his healing and could testify, "Most people who have had leukemia don't go around talking about it—they have passed on. Thank God, there is no sickness He cannot heal."

"He Shall Quicken Your Mortal Bodies"

Lowell Ashbrook had not planned to preach a sermon to himself that Easter morning in 1958. He began by reading Romans 8:11, "He that raised up Christ from the dead shall also quicken your mortal bodies by his Spirit that dwelleth in you." But as he began to apply the truth of the resurrection, which will occur at the rapture of the Church, he suddenly saw a truth he had not noticed before: God would quicken our *mortal* bodies, not only in the resurrection but now. He would heal our sicknesses.

As he continued his sermon, Ashbrook began praying in his heart for himself, *O God, Your Spirit dwells in me. Now quicken this mortal body of mine.*

The speaker had a very good reason to pray this way. Less than seven weeks before, during exploratory surgery, surgeons had found a large malignant tumor wrapped around his bronchial tubes. The other organs were so involved that the tumor could not be removed. Also it was a secondary cancer, meaning it had begun elsewhere then spread to this area.

Three weeks after the surgery, the doctor wanted to begin the usual treatments, such as X-ray therapy and nitrogen mustard shots. The patient asked, "What will it do for me?"

"If we are lucky," the doctor said, "and we think we will be, we may give you three years of activity."

"Will it make me well?" Ashbrook asked.

"No, it won't," was the reply.

"In other words, Doctor, if I get well, God's going to have to do it."

"That's about it," he replied.

Lowell Ashbrook gave his decision to the physician, "My wife and I knew you would suggest this therapy, Doctor, so we have already discussed it. We decided that if it happens, God has to do it; we will not complicate matters with treatments."

The doctor said he would stand ready to help anytime he was needed. He must have thought Ashbrook was going to go home to get in bed and die of the disease.

Ashbrook was superintendent of the Assemblies of God Louisiana District, and the churches and people rallied behind him in prayer support as he continued his duties. He had preached five weeks after the exploratory surgery, and now, two weeks later, God had quickened this text to his heart.

Healing did not come immediately. The struggle lasted three years. In fact, in the summer of 1958, a large, painful swelling developed under his left arm. He felt it scores of times each day and discouragement attacked him.

During a meeting in Arkansas, Mrs. G. W. Hardcastle, wife of the superintendent of the Arkansas district, noticed Ashbrook's depression and asked the reason. When he told her of the painful lump, she advised him not to "satisfy the devil by feeling under your arm." He took her advice. Several weeks later he noticed the lump was gone.

There were other tests, but the Ashbrooks kept claiming the promise God had made real that Easter morning. As time went on, the symptoms of cancer disappeared. After retirement from his post as superintendent, he and his wife, Edna, had a productive ministry traveling as missionary-evangelists to fifty-eight countries. While pastoring in the international city of Hong

Kong, ministering to hundreds of people each Sunday, they witnessed great outpourings of the Holy Spirit.

At the time of this report, more than thirty-five years had gone by since the doctor's grim prediction of only three years of life. Physicians were astounded at Lowell Ashbrook's recovery and had no natural explanation. God had fulfilled His promise and quickened his mortal body.

Healed of Multiple Sclerosis

In the early part of August 1993, Donna Tilley began experiencing some disturbing symptoms. The bottoms of her feet had a burning sensation, and her legs felt very heavy and were constantly numb. After a couple of weeks she was suffering from severe fatigue and had begun to walk with a limp. It hindered her work with her husband, Gary, as administrators for The People's Church of Arnold, Missouri.

Donna went to an internist, Dr. Wilke, who began extensive testing and listed four possible diseases, then recommended that she check with a neurologist. She was not prepared for what Dr. Carpenter told her on August 27, that in his judgment she had multiple sclerosis.

"I couldn't even say multiple sclerosis, much less spell it," Donna says, "but I soon became very educated." The doctor told her the outlook was bleak. There were three possibilities for her: (1) work with some discomfort, (2) work but be noticeably impaired, or (3) become housebound and confined to a wheelchair. Remission was possible, but there was no treatment that could bring healing.

It seemed as though the third possibility would be her lot. Her legs were getting weaker, she could not work a full day, and she had to rely on others to help with housework and shopping. She was becoming a prisoner of this dreaded disease. Depression settled down on her, and she feared the future.

God began to work with Donna, however, putting in her heart a desire to draw closer to Him, the Healer, instead of seeking the healing.

On Tuesday night, September 21, during services with evangelist John Davis, those with MS were encouraged to come to the prayer line. It was a struggle for Donna to do so, but she did, and as she was singing with others the chorus "Look What the Lord Has Done," strength began returning to her legs.

Just a few days earlier Donna had tried to run in private and could not do so, but that Tuesday night she could not refrain from running or dancing. She was up until midnight, her strength had returned, and she says, "The next morning I was still bouncing."

From that time she was able to walk normally, with no limp, and to work a full schedule, with no fatigue.

Postscript: The church had made unusual spiritual preparations for the revival meetings. On September 13, Pastor Kenneth Brown called the congregation to a time of fasting. They could choose a fast of all media (TV, radio, newspapers); a limited fast of one, two, or three meals per day; or a "Daniel fast" of only bread and water. Some did not eat a bite of food from Monday to Sunday.

The climax was a total fast recommended for twenty-four hours from sundown, Monday, September 20, until after the Tuesday evening service on September 21. In addition to Donna Tilley (the pastor's daughter) many others found healing in that Tuesday evening service.

The Writing on the Wall

Nineteen sixty-eight was a distressful time for Joanne Ohlin. She was deeply involved in the work of her husband, John, as youth and Christian education director for the Wisconsin-Northern Michigan District of the Assemblies of God, and presently he was overseeing the summer youth camps. He had received an invitation to accept a position at the Assemblies of God Headquarters in Springfield, Missouri. It appeared to be a splendid opportunity for them to enlarge their scope of ministry, but one facet of their lives was causing them great concern. Should they make a move when their daughter was in such poor health?

Earlier that year, thirteen-year-old Cheri had become seriously ill. Specialists at a Marshfield, Wisconsin, clinic had diagnosed her problem as chronic glomerulonephritis, a form of kidney inflammation. She was immediately placed in a hospital for further tests, including a kidney biopsy, to determine the extent of the damage.

When the parents brought Cheri home, the doctors told them

she could survive a few years of life but on a very restricted basis. They prescribed a strict, salt-free, high-protein diet plus twenty pills a day, taken around the clock at three-hour intervals.

It was such a strong dosage that the first time a pharmacist saw the prescription, he was sure there had been a mistake and would not fill it until he had made a long-distance phone call to verify that the prescription was correct.

The drugs immediately produced very disagreeable side effects for Cheri. They caused such swelling that some friends did not recognize her; sometimes her eyes were swollen shut. The weekly trips to the clinic never resulted in good reports.

At the family doctor's suggestion, John and Joanne transferred their daughter to a hospital in Madison, where she endured additional tests and another kidney biopsy. Despite the stringent diet and medication there was no improvement.

So that night at youth camp Joanne was understandably discouraged and began questioning, "Lord, why does this have to happen to us?"

One night, after the rest of the family had retired, she slipped into Cheri's room. With tears flowing down her face she pleaded with the Lord to heal their daughter and to give them some sign of encouragement. Above all, she prayed that His name might be glorified through this testing time.

At that moment a friend, Mrs. Elmer Bilton, stopped by to pray with her. The Lord had impressed her that the parents needed special encouragement.

After the friend left, Joanne sat down to read her Bible and a few chapters from a book on faith. It was hard to concentrate, so she returned to her bedroom.

There on the wall in clear handwriting she was startled to see: "Psalm 41:2."

Turning to this verse in her Bible, Joanne read, "The Lord will preserve him, and keep him alive; and he shall be blessed upon the earth: and thou wilt not deliver him unto the will of his enemies." The Lord impressed her to change the masculine nouns to feminine and that they applied to Cheri. The entire psalm was a tremendous encouragement.

When God wrote on the wall in Daniel's time, it was a message of judgment. This time it was a message of mercy and hope. The heavy load lifted from Joanne, and from that moment she had the assurance Cheri would be healed. Though the healing did not come immediately, and there were tests of their faith, God's promise was a constant companion to uphold and encourage.

The doctor agreed that the medication was of no help, so he gradually reduced it, and Cheri began eating everything she wanted. After the family moved to Springfield, Cheri was taken for periodic checkups, tests, and biopsies. With each visit the doctor noticed marked improvement and stated her recovery was unusual. Over and over he said, "I can't understand it. We aren't doing anything. I am just amazed."

In May 1972 Cheri made her final visit to a specialist. The father began to thank him for what he had done, but the doctor interrupted, "We haven't done anything. We just sat back and watched the miracle take place. It is certainly true that a Greater Power than ours intervened in this case." He declared her completely well and said she need not return anymore.

Postscript: The story of Cheri's healing was included in materials provided for the National Women's Ministries Day observance in February 1978. Sharon Sparling of Webster, New York, wrote in September of the effect the story had on her life. The Monday before the Women's Ministries Day service, she had undergone surgery for a malignant tumor. The surgeon found the cancer had spread to her liver and lymph glands in her abdominal area and gave her only a short time to live. She was only thirty-five at the time and still had two children at home.

A friend sent Sharon a copy of the testimony and wrote, "The Lord is no respecter of persons—we can ask as much for you."

As Sharon read Psalm 41:2, the Lord made it real to her, His peace swept over her, and she appropriated the promise for herself. A few days later Jeremiah 30:17 was made real: "I will restore health unto thee, and I will heal thee of thy wounds." She, her family, and many friends in the church prayed earnestly.

Sharon regained strength so rapidly she was able to attend a statewide Easter youth convention five weeks later. On Good Friday evening there was a great move of the Holy Spirit, and many received healing. She also felt the power of God upon her from head to foot, especially in the stomach area. She had many medical tests after that time and all showed her to be healed.

(Maybe this testimony will inspire someone else to believe God for a miracle.)

Just Six Weeks to Live

In his book *Kathryn Kuhlman: The Woman Behind the*

Miracles, Wayne Warner tells about one of the many healings that occurred during the ministry of the late evangelist. It includes unplanned participation by a well-known entertainer, Phyllis Diller.

In 1967 Mrs. Marjorie Close of Greensburg, Pennsylvania—not far from Pittsburgh where Miss Kuhlman conducted services—received some startling and frightening news after exploratory surgery. Her surgeon, Dr. Parrone, told her she had stomach cancer and gave her only about six weeks to live. "I've cut the diseased parts away," he said. "Now it's up to you and the Man upstairs."

Marjorie, raised in the Church of Christ, knew very little about divine healing, but a friend's contact with Miss Diller, one of Marjorie's favorite entertainers, awakened her interest. The comedienne sent an autographed photo and recommended three books for her to read. One was Kuhlman's *I Believe in Miracles*.

With death only weeks away, Marjorie Close was looking for help anywhere. Sent home to die, her weight had dropped to ninety-seven pounds. She was too ill to cook, and even walking to the grocery story one block away required two rest stops coming and going. The pain in her mouth and throat was so excruciating she could hardly swallow.

Another person appeared on the scene. Larry Ahlborn, a local gospel pianist and singer, had been converted several years earlier under Kathryn Kuhlman's ministry and had begun organizing chartered buses for those wanting to attend the meetings in Pittsburgh.

He tried to enlist Marjorie to go on one of the trips. Four times she agreed, then withdrew, fearing she might get involved in fanaticism. When Larry invited her for the fifth time, Marjorie Close accepted and got on the bus with her daughter Janie. Even after they were on the road to Pittsburgh she thought she had made a mistake and told Janie perhaps they should get off the bus.

"No," Janie replied, "we've come this far, and we might as well go on to Pittsburgh."

Throughout Kathryn Kuhlman's services, she encouraged people to believe God for healing. They didn't have to wait for the evangelist to pray for them. True to the pattern, God did something for Marjorie Close before any call came for people to come forward. She suddenly experienced a warm sensation coming over her head and then to her stomach. She also noticed that a lemon-size lump had disappeared from her stomach.

One of the ushers sensed that something had happened and encouraged Marjorie to go to the stage and testify. "I wasn't even born again at the time," Mrs. Close said, although she thought she was a Christian because she belonged to a church. When Kathryn learned she was not converted, she led her in the sinner's prayer.

Next, Kathryn touched both the mother and daughter, and both fell to the floor. (This was a phenomenon in Kathryn's meetings that she called "being slain in the Spirit." Often when she touched people, their knees would buckle and they would fall to the floor or into the waiting arms of an usher.)

Of the experience Mrs. Close said, "It seemed like I was in another world. It was the most marvelous feeling I had ever had. I saw everything in a beautiful, bright light."

When Marjorie Close left for home, it was not only with a healed body but a changed heart. "I no longer hated people," she said. "I loved everyone. It seemed like I had been washed inside and out. Completely."

Marjorie proved the reality of her healing when she arrived home at Greensburg. She walked the six blocks to her house, uphill and down, without having to rest once. Then she did something she had been unable to do for two years: she prepared dinner for her family—spaghetti and two lemon pies—and sat down and ate it with them.

Her family had some reservations at first—had she become mixed up with a fanatical religion? But as she obeyed Kathryn Kuhlman's advice to just go home and live the life, to "let God do His own work," her family saw God in her and eventually came to know Him just as she did.

Even the doctor was convinced of the miracle when Marjorie returned for a checkup, going so far as to correspond with Kathryn Kuhlman, adding to her ministry files a before-and-after letter about Marjorie's case.

Victory over Cancer

Early in 1977 Mary Lou Atkins of Thousand Oaks, California,

44

had a severe test of her faith. She had always been healthy and strong, with no major illnesses or surgeries.

Now she noticed her abdomen had become enlarged and had an unusual firmness. One doctor told her she appeared to be six months pregnant. After numerous examinations and procedures, he told her she must have exploratory surgery and a hysterectomy. There were no other symptoms of a problem except the enlarged stomach.

It was a different story, however, when Mary Lou's doctor, Robert Brown, performed the surgery. She was diagnosed as having ovarian cancer at stage three (of four stages). The cancer had spread beyond the ovaries to other body parts inside the abdomen.

The doctors did what they could, then recommended to her family and to her pastor that they enjoy her companionship as much as possible, for she had about six months to live. With chemotherapy she might live two years.

Immediately, her family and friends went to prayer on her behalf. There was marked improvement almost instantly. At the time of surgery she had been very pale, but in a short time her color returned, and she did not appear to have been sick at all.

Even the monthly chemotherapy treatments did not affect her adversely. They did not cause stomach sickness, which is usually the case, and she did not lose her hair. Also, Dr. Brown's prognosis that she would go into early menopause did not prove accurate.

After two years Mary Lou felt so much stronger she asked to be taken off the chemotherapy treatments. Her doctor said he would need to perform another surgery to see her condition. After doing so he reported that Mary Lou was cured. At the time of this writing, seventeen years had passed, and she was still well.

Prayed for on Behalf of Her Granddaughter

In the early 1950s Delmer Guynes's daughter Rebecca, one and a half years of age, began to become listless and had no appetite. Eventually she had to be carried about by her parents, and it seemed evident she would die without some relief. The family doctor could not determine the cause.

The situation was becoming serious. While attending a church

45

service, Rebecca's grandmother felt impressed to go forward to be anointed and prayed for on behalf of her dying grandchild.

An amazing transformation occurred. Sometime that evening or early the next morning, Rebecca was miraculously healed. Her vigor and appetite returned, and she began running about the house.

A short time later the Guynes family learned the cause of the problem, what it was, and proof of the healing. Delmer Guynes's father was diagnosed as having infectious tuberculosis, so the parents immediately had Rebecca tested for infection. The tests showed conclusively that she had been seriously infected and had had two large spots on her lungs. However, the spots were now healed completely, and the infection was entirely gone.

Forty years later Rebecca and her husband, David D. Smith, are serving their fifth term as missionaries in Kenya, East Africa. She has also experienced deliverance from a cancerous condition, which left her with only a few months to live, and other physical problems as well. (Delmer R. Guynes is president of Southwestern Assemblies of God College, Waxahachie, Texas.)

Multiple Healings

In the early 1990s, Pastor Darrell Roberts of Logan, New Mexico, had received one blow after another concerning his physical condition. For several months he had not felt well and finally went to a doctor on a Monday. Preliminary tests indicated diabetes, and the doctor made a Friday appointment to discover the extent of the problem. However, Pastor Roberts' difficulties increased rapidly.

That Monday night a severe headache tortured him. Though prayer brought relief, he was not prepared for what happened on Wednesday morning, when he awoke with a terrible pain in his neck. It would continue for two weeks, and the day of his appointment it was almost unbearable. Also, that Friday morning he discovered the right side of his face was paralyzed. His doctor sent him to the emergency room of the hospital, where it was determined his facial problem was caused by Bell's palsy, a condition that would require the body to heal itself.

The picture became even darker after he returned to his own doctor, who reported on the tests. His cholesterol and triglyceride levels were so high the doctor's machine could not measure them.

The levels would need to be checked at a larger hospital in Albuquerque. The tests also showed his liver was enlarged, his pancreas was not functioning properly—in fact, the doctor believed he had pancreatic cancer.

The blood samples sent to Albuquerque had to be diluted for the tests because the blood was so full of fat it clouded the machinery. The tests showed his cholesterol level (on a scale that considers 240 poor) was 900, and the triglyceride level (on a scale that considers 181 poor) was 4,900!

But God heard the prayers of local friends, who came and prayed for Pastor Roberts on Saturday, as well as others across the country whom they had called. He reported, "On Sunday I woke up with joy. The physical symptoms that had plagued me for two years were gone, and they have not returned."

The next day after more blood tests were given, the doctor was astounded at the results. He said, "I know you have been praying. Something miraculous has taken place." God had healed his pancreatic cancer. The enlarged liver was now normal and the cancer had disappeared.

Pastor Roberts wondered why the blood levels were still high and the paralysis still present. Perhaps the reason became apparent after his doctor transferred him to an Amarillo hospital for further tests. He was able to witness to a backslidden intern who was assigned to his case and to his roommate who was trying to overcome an alcohol problem.

Within a week the blood count numbers had plummeted, the paralysis gradually disappeared, and his sugar count returned to just about normal.

About a year and a half after Darrell Roberts' healing, the doctors decided they needed to check the condition of his arteries, since they might be clogged because of the former high cholesterol level. When they did the test, he heard the doctor say, "I can't believe this; his arteries are 100 percent open, just like a newborn baby."

A Surprise Healing

Seventy-eight-year-old Mamie Dinkens was a good Baptist—in fact, she had been the wife of a Baptist preacher—and had not been convinced of healing or other supernatural experiences. So she was very surprised at what happened at Calvary Temple

(Yuba City, California) on Sunday evening, December 13, 1992.

Five years earlier she had begun having trouble with her one eye (she had lost sight in the other eye at the age of two). Light caused it to hurt so badly that by nightfall she would cover it with a cloth. The crisis arrived when her doctor told her she had a cataract and needed an operation. The thought of losing her sight, even temporarily, pushed her into hysterical crying.

Mamie began to pray for peace of mind and assurance of God's will, and He did more for her than she asked. That night in 1992 the lights at the church hurt so much she had to close her eye.

Then, prompted by the Holy Spirit, the pastor called for anyone who had any fear to come forward for deliverance.

Mamie felt a voice inside telling her that if she would respond she would get relief, so she went forward.

But the next thing she knew she was on the floor, overcome by the power of God's presence. Her husband could not even hold her up. Neither one had ever experienced anything like this before.

There came to Mamie a tremendous sense of peace. When some people finally lifted her to her feet, her fear was completely gone. She still did not know what had happened. She was so lost to her surroundings that her daughter had to ask several times if she could see. She found she was healed. She could look directly into the lights with no pain.

Mamie Dinkens was a surprised woman. She said, "I'm a Baptist, and we don't believe in these things!" But she went on to say, "God showed me He is here. . . . He truly answered my prayer."

A Child Saved from Blindness

In January 1992 Gary and Karma Nelson of Duncombe, Iowa, received some disturbing news about their daughter April. Their concern had begun in the spring of 1991 when she was ten years old. Her fourth-grade teacher had noticed some changes in her behavior. Normally energetic and loving, April was beginning to show frustration and anger, and her grades were dropping.

Looking for clues to the problem, her parents noticed April held books very close to her eyes when she read; she also tilted her head when watching TV. Thinking she might need glasses, the parents took their daughter for an eye examination.

That is when the doctor gave his diagnosis that April had an inherited eye disorder: Stargardt's macular degeneration. It is also known as juvenile hereditary macular dystrophy. A second opinion at a well-known university hospital confirmed the diagnosis. April's central vision would continue to deteriorate. Her vision at the testing was 20/70, and this condition usually results in a drop of vision to 20/200 or 20/300, which is legal blindness.

Devastated by this news, prayer was the family's recourse. Other believers, the church, April's Christian school, and people in churches all over the country united in prayer for the child's deliverance. She began to suffer stomach pains and migraine headaches but through it all believed God would heal her.

In June 1992 April was scheduled to get magnifying glasses to help her deteriorating vision, although she was determined not to use them. She was trusting God.

"What have you been doing for your daughter's eyes?" the doctor asked after the test.

The parents told him they had been praying.

"Just your family?" he asked.

They told him people all over the country had been praying for April.

Then came wonderful news. In five months April's vision had improved from 20/70 to 20/30! April needed no glasses.

The parents continued to pray for a completed work, and on August 20, 1992, their daughter's eyes tested 20/20.

The doctor could find no medical reason for the total change. Cases like this were not supposed to improve. She was healed of her stomach pains and migraine headaches as well.

God's Nudge in the Night

It was devastating news that came to Betty Jane Grams, longtime missionary to Latin America, that day in 1956. The doctor at the American Clinic in La Paz, Bolivia, announced, "Your baby cannot live through the night. Her lungs have not opened."

Betty Jane knew that in the high, thin air at thirteen thousand feet above sea level, babies often died, even those born to the Aymara people, who are used to the climate. A baby born to another missionary that month had already died. What hope was there for little Rachel?

Neither Betty Jane nor her husband, Monroe, had told relatives in the United States that they were expecting a child. It had been a difficult pregnancy with several complications. Now, after hours of labor, the baby had arrived, presenting them with this emergency.

Both the father and mother were exhausted from many trips in the rugged mountain country. Betty Jane had been teaching, playing the piano, and ministering right up to the hour she had gone to the hospital. Worn out, both parents needed strength for this spiritual battle.

"Call my husband; we must pray together," Betty Jane told the nurse. When he came in, the focus of their prayer was, "Lord, lay our need on the heart of someone back home in America."

Fortunately, God is not limited to office hours but is available twenty-four hours a day. The Grams learned later how God had answered.

Betty Jane received a letter from Monroe's sister. She asked, "What is your need? I dreamed that I saw Monroe pacing the floor with a baby in his arms. Startled, I woke up and prayed in the Spirit."

Although she had not known they were expecting a child, God had nudged her awake and told her of their need.

Betty Jane's mother wrote that a longtime friend had been burdened for them. While at her nighttime job as a custodian cleaning an office, in response to a nudge from God, she had interceded in the Spirit for the Grams.

Though two women were eight thousand miles away from La Paz, God had nudged them, putting in their hearts the need to pray.

Did God answer the prayers He had inspired? Back in La Paz, the doctor came to the mother's bedside. "Señora Grams," he exclaimed, "something strange has happened. Your baby is still alive. We have put her on the pulmotor, and she is rallying."

"We are praying," was the mother's quiet answer.

After little Rachel had been on the pulmotor several days, the night nurse responded to the pleading of the mother, who had not seen her baby yet, and brought her in. She was all swaddled up, as is the custom with babies in the Bolivian highlands. Betty Jane carefully inspected her, then handed her back. She knew her baby would live.

At this reporting of their story, the Grams' daughter had grown to maturity, graduated from North Central Bible College, received many honors, was the mother of three girls, and was in ministry with her husband, Steve Schaible.

"Divine Intervention—No Question"

Kenneth and Doris Brown sat stunned that early Sunday morning in 1989. As busy pastors at The People's Church in Arnold, Missouri, they were currently involved in a marriage seminar, and there was to be a wedding that afternoon, but now the grim news from the doctor became top priority.

Until now, Pastor Brown's needing a doctor's assistance had been minimal, but recent developments had forced him to have an examination at St. Joseph's Hospital, St. Louis, Missouri. For some weeks blood from his left nostril on his pillow and face in the mornings had alerted him that something was wrong.

He was not prepared, however, for the physician's announcement after a 5:30 A.M. examination, "I'm sorry to tell you that you have cancer."

After further tests the rest of the morning, Brown asked the doctor how soon he wanted to perform the surgery. The reply showed the urgency of the situation—"Today if I can get a surgery room." The tests had revealed ethmoid carcinoma, which is usually found in the intestines but almost never in the sinus area.

"D day" for the brain surgery was to be Thursday, four days later. The pastor entered the hospital on Wednesday for a battery of tests and other preparations. The family and church congregation engaged in fervent prayer. More than sixty people were at the hospital during the surgery, praying and waiting to learn the results.

It was not to be a typical surgery. There was concern the cancer might have invaded Rev. Brown's voice box. Various doctors explained they would be working very near the optic nerve, and there was the possibility of blindness in one or both eyes. As Rev. Brown spoke to each member of his family, he realized it might be the last time he would see them in this life.

It is good to know Christ at a time like this. As the pastor prayed, "Jesus, please help me," He calmed the man's pounding heart.

The surgery lasted nearly eleven hours. The family had been prepared to find the patient with swollen eyes, confusion, severe headaches, and irritability. Amazingly, within the limitations of a respirator, he could see, reason, and communicate.

There was a long period of convalescence, but the magnitude of God's help became known sometime later when the surgeon told Doris Brown, "I have performed five surgeries of this kind since Pastor Brown's, and he is the only survivor."

A statement to Rev. Kenneth Brown from Dr. Philip L. Martin says, "It has been five years since our team removed the adeno-carcinoma from your ethmoid sinus. At the one-year post-op I considered your survival divine intervention. At five years I don't think there's any question."

"Rise and Walk"

Because she was a nurse, Ethyl (Mrs. Lloyd) Humphrey of St. Joseph, Missouri, knew exactly what was wrong with her. She had a cardiac condition and other complications. The heart problem had begun about seven years earlier but gradually grew worse due to overwork. A blockage in her heart prevented the normal flow of blood from one chamber to another. The heart had become enlarged to the point where it resembled a long-necked gourd; it reached from the ribs on the left side to far beyond the midline on the right and depressed the diaphragm.

Instead of the normal cadence of the heart, she had a gallop rhythm most of the time, causing pain that extended down the left arm, through the chest, and up the left side of her neck.

Ethyl also had cardiac asthma, caused by the heart problem. The lung tissues would fill with fluid, making breathing almost impossible. To dehydrate the fluid, she was given hypodermics and placed under oxygen after each attack.

Another complication was nephritis, a failure of the kidney function—in her case, her kidneys were only 35 percent of nor-mal. This led to arthritis from the pelvis downward, which was so severe she was unable to walk.

For over seven months, from August 3, 1950, to March 18, 1951, Mrs. Humphrey was bedfast. The physicians had given her up, saying that medication could no longer help her and that she had only a short time to live.

Palm Sunday 1952 was a date to be remembered. Learning that evangelist Louise Nankivell was conducting gospel meet-ings in the city, Ethyl asked to be taken to one, for the evangelist was praying for the sick. An ambulance was needed, and the patient had so much difficulty breathing she had to have someone fan her, and water was brought to help revive her somewhat. Louise Nankivell prayed for Mrs. Humphrey, and within a few minutes her breathing improved. Then the evangelist said, "Place your hands in those of your Savior, and if He tells you to walk, get up and walk."

Ethyl waited a few minutes, then it seemed she heard Christ say to her, *Rise and walk*. At first several ushers had to help her, but soon she was walking alone.

The change in Nurse Ethyl Humphrey was remarkable. Those who saw her when she entered the building said her face had the gray pallor of death on it, and her eyes were sunken. Several of her former patients who were present said that when she left, her face wore a rosy hue.

Soon she was walking everywhere, and the former conditions that had threatened her life disappeared. When she was checked by her physician and the tests proved her healing, he said, "It is wonderful indeed."

Gunshot Wound Turned Him Around

In 1958 no one would have prophesied that Patrick Donadio would become a minister of the gospel and eventually be the national secretary for Mission America Placement Service, an important ministry of the Assemblies of God. In his early twenties, he was unsaved and running with a wild crowd in New York City. Only one factor forecast anything for his future except a life of crime and probably prison: he had praying parents and a praying pastor.

But that night in October 1958, Patrick Donadio was not considering a change in his lifestyle. With three other young men, he was engaged in an armed robbery. He says, "We had been pilfering this area for about two weeks, which was not too smart because the police had set a trap for us."

When they arrived at the crime scene, Patrick glimpsed a police car, yelled to his companions, and they began running through a wooded area back to their car. Glancing back over his shoulder as he ran, Patrick saw a policeman steadying himself against a tree and holding his pistol with both hands. From experience the youth knew his chances of being hit were great.

A shot rang out, and a bullet penetrated Patrick's hip, felling him and causing extreme pain. But no bone was broken, so he was able to get up and begin running again. Another shot hit him in his left leg, and once more he fell, only to get up and continue toward the car. Even though he was hit two more times and was bleeding profusely, he made it to the car.

Because their car was parked on a road parallel to the one the police car was on, with no crossroads connecting them, they were able to escape. However, Patrick was in a critical condition, for he was bleeding to death in the backseat. Fortunately for him, the car was stopped for speeding, and one of the young men said Patrick had been injured in a hunting accident; the officer escorted them to a hospital. On the way the officer contacted Patrick's parents, and they were waiting when he arrived.

The prognosis was bad. Patrick had lost most of his blood, his veins had collapsed, and his heart was practically pumping air. The doctors told his parents they expected him to die.

The patient's father knew what to do. He called the pastor of the church the family attended, Mary Corvene. The parents knew that she was a woman of prayer. Their only hope was God.

Patrick was in intensive care for thirty-one days, and the doctors found it hard to believe he had survived. One, Dr. Cerasono, said, "Young man, as sure as there is a God in heaven, He pulled you through this ordeal." He said he had not seen gunshot wounds as bad as these since World War II.

But prospects were still not good for Patrick. The doctor said that though his life had been spared, he would never walk on that leg again, he would drag it like a cripple, and when he turned his body around, he would have to pick up his leg with his hands and turn the leg. The best thing to do, he said, would be to amputate the leg and get an artificial one. At least he would be able to walk straight.

Responding, Patrick's father told the doctor, "We have trusted the Lord this far; we're going to trust Him all the way."

God answered the prayers of godly people. More than thirty-five years later, Patrick Donadio could report, "My leg is normal today. I walk perfectly, and I even played football in college."

Six Operations—Then Victory

It looked like life was about over for Ione Soltau, dean of

women at North Central Bible College in Minneapolis, Minnesota. The doctor's diagnosis was that her cancer was terminal.

The struggle began in 1959. She says, "Little did I realize as I closed my office door that August 30, that the Lord was ushering me into a very different box of my life." Three times in the next few weeks she found herself quoting Psalm 23 ("The Lord Is My Shepherd"). Then each time before six surgeries she repeated that psalm to herself.

Prayer sustained Ione, and each time her recovery surprised her two doctors, who were fine Christians and gave credit to God. One of them told Ione before her fifth operation, "What your God has done before, He can do again."

Then in 1963, Ione was admitted to the hospital once more and underwent a sixth operation. This time the doctors told her they could do no more for her. The cancer could not be surgically removed. The verdict was metastasis, cancer in the bloodstream.

Friends surrounded Ione with prayer. More than forty-five pastors and their wives visited and prayed for her. Her church, the college, and friends across the country held prayer meetings to pray for her. Some at times prayed around the clock.

God answered prayer, though the healing came slowly. She continued as dean of women at the college for years; she has been a teacher of art and has had her own showings. She has been a popular speaker at summer camps, children's crusades, and churches. The healing was indeed a new beginning for her.

Thirty years later, in 1993, Ione Soltau was still free of cancer and still active. Every time one of her doctors sees her, he says, "You are my miracle. I must believe in a God of miracles."

Ione says, "Every added day of living is an adventure in serving the Lord."

Prayer Prevents Amputation

The phone call from Debbie, who stayed with eighty-eight-year-old Irene Falen—a widow from Topeka, Kansas—alarmed Irene's daughter, Lenore Edoff. The young woman reported that the elderly Falen's left leg had become swollen and red and was quite a bit warmer than her right leg. It was decided to take her to the emergency room of the hospital.

The daughter was surprised that the doctor on duty paid very little attention to the left leg after finding no pulse in her right foot or venous vein. He told the two women that the condition was not good; he was sure an amputation would be necessary. In fact, he wanted to call for a vascular surgeon to perform the operation.

The women were stunned at such a report, but Debbie immediately phoned Glad Tidings Assembly of God, where the mother was a longtime member. Pastor Ron Pettet and youth pastor Kevin Roach arrived in a few minutes and prayed for the patient before the surgeon arrived.

Something marvelous happened. The surgeon found a pulse and evidence of circulation. Irene Falen recovered from the inflammation in the left leg and had use of both legs until she went to be with the Lord almost three years later, in 1992.

"Diseased in His Feet"

During his second term of missionary service in Africa, Robert Webb began suffering from a severe infection in his feet. He says, "If you can imagine athlete's foot becoming extremely infected, you can begin to understand my pain and suffering."

The ailment had occurred because of his having to baptize in contaminated water. The policy in Nigeria restricted baptizing to missionaries or African pastors who were ordained. And in Western Nigeria in 1963, there were many converts but few ordained pastors; consequently, much of the baptizing fell to Webb.

In addition to the intense pain, bad enough in itself, Satan attacked the missionary's mind. It seemed he constantly accused, *You are wasting your life and the money from your supporters*. He had to battle discouragement every day.

A policy of asking ministers to report on their work—a "taking accounts day"—is one of the great reasons for the growth and revival in Nigeria. It brought a crisis to Webb, however, for as supervisor of the work in that area, he was the one the ministers would report to. For them to see a sick and suffering missionary on "accounts day" would not bring glory to God, he felt.

He sought for a Scripture verse on which to base his faith for healing, and the day before the African pastors were to arrive, he picked up in his office a booklet written by A. B. Simpson, *The Gospel of Healing*. (Simpson, an early leader of the Christian and

Missionary Alliance, was active around the turn of the century in pioneering faith in God for healing.)

The Lord brought to Webb's attention what Simpson wrote about King Asa, who was "diseased in his feet" (2 Chronicles 16:12–14). The Bible states Asa was not healed because "he sought not to the Lord."

Robert Webb believed God had spoken to him, wanting to heal him. Prompted by God, he asked the African ministers to lay hands on him and pray for his affliction.

"Immediately after their fervent prayer," Webb reports, "my feet began to heal," and he became completely well. An added result: the African pastors became more active in praying for the sick than they had been. This, in turn, was a major reason for the growth in the number of churches in Nigeria—from five in 1963 to more than two hundred in 1993.

No Pulse, No Heartbeat

The doctors of Mt. Carmel Catholic Hospital in Pittsburg, Kansas, finally gave up on eight-year-old Dorothy Smitley that summer of 1939. She had come in on Wednesday, July 12, for emergency surgery. But some days later her fever had reached 108.4 degrees, a record for the hospital. Because of the high fever, Doctors C. H. Smith and J. H. Bena told her parents that the brain cells would be burned up, and she would be a vegetable.

The ordeal had begun for Dorothy on July 4 with stomach pains. Her parents did not consider the possibility of appendicitis, for the pain was opposite the usual location.

To the family's dismay, however, when she was taken to the hospital, the physicians discovered Dorothy's appendix had indeed ruptured, and gangrene and pernicious peritonitis had set in. So on July 12 the doctors performed emergency surgery. After the operation the patient lay for days in the hospital, fed through the veins.

Dorothy's condition became critical. She had no pulse or heartbeat. Because death seemed so imminent, the pillows and flowers had been removed from the room. Her situation appeared to be hopeless.

However, Dorothy's parents had a source of help that many people do not know. As pastors of the Pittsburg, Kansas, Assembly of God, they were praying people. At the crisis hour, when her fever reached 108 degrees about two o'clock on a Friday morning, they began phoning for prayer assistance. They called Assemblies of God leaders at the headquarters city, Springfield, Missouri—W. I. Evans, Noel Perkin, and J. R. Flower—and other people across the nation.

Either the father or the mother had remained at their daughter's bedside continuously. After making the phone calls, the father returned to Dorothy's room and resumed his prayer vigil. He prayed for strength and put her in the hands of God.

Then the miracle happened. Suddenly Dorothy's eyes opened as she regained consciousness. Her heart and pulse resumed their normal rhythm, and her temperature began to drop. In less than an hour it dropped seven degrees, from the 108.4 mark to 101!

Her legs were a continuing problem. Because they had been extended for so long, propped up with pillows so she could receive shots, they had become completely stiff. According to the doctors, she would never walk again, and they considered cutting some tendons so she could be in a sitting position. This would mean confinement to a wheelchair the rest of her life.

Dorothy's parents could not agree to this. Over a period of time, through physical therapy, she recovered the use of her legs. She had to learn to walk a second time, but her legs became normal.

At the time of writing this, fifty-five years later, Dorothy (Smitley) Bagwell could report she is the mother of five healthy children and still busy in church work and various kinds of recreational activities. Her walking is normal, and she has had a successful career as a secretary for a bridge-building company, never showing any signs of the brain damage the doctors had predicted.

Section Two

Special Miracles

God wrought special miracles.—Acts 19:11

Miracles are special demonstrations of the power of God. The Old Testament relates a multitude of them that are so powerful they must be explained as demonstrations of God's power, for example, making a path through the Red Sea, providing food and water for Israel for forty years, the victory at Jericho, and the sun standing still.

Jesus' ministry also contained miracles, such as turning water into wine and raising people from the dead—He raised Jairus's daughter, the son of the widow of Nain, and Lazarus, after being dead four days.

Jesus told His disciples that they would do the works He did and even greater after He returned to the Father (John 14:12). This power was not to glorify them but a means to bear witness unto Him (Acts 1:8).

It seems a pattern of history, as Stanley Horton states, "God often uses a miracle as a wedge, to open a new door for the proclamation of the gospel."

The healing of the man lame from birth in Acts 3 is called "a notable miracle" in 4:16.

Some scholars believe the mention of Peter's shadow in 5:15 implies people were healed by that means.

The people of Samaria listened to Philip's preaching about Jesus because they saw "the miracles which he did" (8:6).

After Philip won the eunuch to the Lord, "the Spirit of the Lord caught away Philip" (8:39).

When Peter was delivered from prison by an angel, his chains fell off, and the huge iron gate that led to the city "opened to them of his own accord" (12:7,10).

When Paul and Silas were in the prison at Philippi, an earthquake occurred, the doors were opened, and the bands of all the prisoners became loose (16:26).

At Ephesus God wrought "special miracles" for Paul, in that cloths from his body brought healing and deliverance from evil spirits (19:11–12).

On the island of Malta, when a snake fastened itself on Paul's hand, the apostle suffered no harm (28:1–5).

Acts Today provides some remarkable instances of miracles God wrought. We gave careful attention to verifying them.

Miracles in Springfield, Missouri

Since many religious denominations trace their beginnings to a single man, it is noteworthy that the Assemblies of God originated because of certain events that caused people to believe God was calling them back to a first-century Christian faith. Supernatural occurrences, beginning in Topeka, Kansas, and culminating in the Azusa Street revival in Los Angeles, produced hundreds of Spirit-filled workers who felt called to spread the good news.

It was at Hot Springs, Arkansas, in April 1914 that the Assemblies of God came into being. The purpose of the founders was to advance the cause by unified action. They could not have known how greatly God would bless their efforts.

Springfield, Missouri, in the Ozarks, figured largely in the development of a Movement based on New Testament principles. The following two accounts tell how God used Spirit-anointed people to foretell the worldwide ministry of the Movement and to claim for God a site that would many years later become the location of the headquarters for the international ministries of the Assemblies of God.

Territory Claimed for God

It was very early on January 1, 1915, when five teenage boys were making their way home after a watch night service of the small congregation that later became Central Assembly in Springfield, Missouri. They included Fred and Paul Corum (their mother, Lillie, was the first person in Springfield to receive the baptism in the Holy Spirit). Also accompanying them was their cousin Laurel Taliaferro, the oldest of the five youths. They were still enjoying the memory of a service in which God had moved upon everyone present.

As they strolled along Campbell Avenue, they came upon the White City Amusement Park, located between Campbell and Boonville and stretching one block north from Lynn to Division. They would never have visited a place known for its worldly activities, but now, noticing some loose boards in the fence, they decided to save time by cutting across to Boonville Avenue. They did not realize they were about to embark on a remarkable journey of faith with far-reaching results.

Fred Corum tells about it in the book *The Sparkling Fountain.* "We regarded it as a den of iniquity, where only the devil and his crowd would want to be." The area was a striking contrast to the holy atmosphere they had just enjoyed.

Suddenly one of the boys spoke up, "This place is unclean!"

Another added, "Do you suppose it could ever belong to God?"

Laurel said, "Let's claim it for God!"

One boy asked, "How much shall we take?"

Another teenager answered, "Let's claim the whole block."

Paul Corum spoke up, "Let's claim the other block too, from Division to Calhoun and Campbell to Boonville."

Fred cautioned, "What about the greenhouse on the corner of Boonville and Calhoun? The owners are nice people."

Laurel settled the matter. "Why not? God will take care of them. Let's claim it *all!*"

So five teenage boys kneeled down and "prayed that all of this land should be used for the work of the Lord so that His gospel might go out to the end of the earth from this place."

Years passed and eventually the site north of Lynn, bordered by Boonville and Campbell, became a ballpark, the home of the Springfield Cardinals. Several outstanding players starred there on their way to the big leagues, including Hall-of-Famer Stan Musial. But then came World War II, entertainment was curtailed, and the site remained unoccupied.

Central Assembly had already bought property at the corner of Campbell and Calhoun (from a saloon keeper), and in the 1950s extended its property to Boonville to make room for a new sanctuary, erected in 1957.

The rapid growth of the Assemblies of God required more room. Its headquarters had moved to Springfield in 1918, locating on West Pacific Street, two blocks north and one block west of the property earlier claimed by the teenagers. The property on Boonville, an ideal site, was procured in 1945. In 1949 Gospel Publishing House moved to the new site and in 1962 the entire headquarters staff made the move.

The boys' act of faith had not yet been fully fulfilled, but as time went on, the rest of the property they had claimed was acquired for the expanding ministries of the denomination. Property on both sides of Boonville and Campbell, and some beyond Division on the north and Calhoun on the south, belongs to Central Assembly or is part of the headquarters complex.

One of the manifestations of the Holy Spirit listed in 1 Corinthians 12 is a special kind of God-given faith (verse 9). Surely it was the Spirit who inspired these young men to take a giant leap of faith. As He often does for His people, God did even more than the youths had believed for, more than they could "ask or imagine" (Ephesians 3:20).

Prophetic Vision

Eight months before the Assemblies of God was founded, God foretold its future, even where its headquarters would be.

He used an evangelist named Rachel Sizelove. She had attended meetings at the famous Azusa Street revival in Los Angeles in 1906 and was baptized in the Holy Spirit there. She had come to Springfield, Missouri, the following year to visit her mother and teach about the baptism; whereupon her sister, Lillie Corum, and others received the same experience. A small group began holding services in homes, store buildings, and tents, but by midsummer 1913, the little church was struggling to survive.

Coming back to Springfield in August 1913, Rachel Sizelove began praying earnestly for the fledgling assembly. As she did so, God gave her a vision. She saw angels coming down and battling for the city. The Lord spoke to the prayer warrior and said, "I'm going to do a work in Springfield that will astonish the world." Then He showed her a vision of a great crystal fountain of pure water bubbling up from the city. Healing waters flowed over the land, spreading to the four points of the compass and covering the entire earth.

Another woman, Amanda E. Benedict, was an important factor in what God did in Springfield. She was well educated and a schoolteacher. Her major ministry was intercession. God placed a burden on her heart for the city of Springfield. Once, obeying what she felt God wanted her to do, she made a pact to sustain herself on only bread and water for a year and spend the time in prayer. Her prayer had a threefold focus: that there would be a Pentecostal church in Springfield, a Pentecostal publishing house, and a Pentecostal Bible school to train ministers.

In *Prophet and a Pen,* Faith Frodsham Campbell's biography of her father, Stanley Frodsham, she states, "My father believed that Central Assembly, Central Bible College, and Gospel Publishing House were largely the results of her [that is, Amanda Benedict's] fervent, effectual prayers."

Rachel Sizelove and Amanda Benedict could not possibly have conceived how wonderfully God would fulfill His promise. About eight months after Rachel Sizelove's vision in April 1914, a group of ministers and laypeople gathered at Hot Springs, Arkansas, to confer. They had received an experience called the baptism in the Holy Spirit, churches were coming into existence in many places, and they wanted a fellowship to conserve the results.

They believed they could accomplish more by working together. They were especially concerned about unifying missionary endeavors, producing literature, and providing proper training for those called into the ministry.

After brief periods of time in Findlay, Ohio, and St. Louis, Missouri, in 1918 the Assemblies of God moved to Springfield, Missouri, and made it their headquarters city.

Beginning in a small building at the corner of West Pacific and Lyon, the work constantly expanded until a large complex on Boonville Avenue became its base of operations.

As a result of the women's prayers, God built a Pentecostal church in Springfield (Central Assembly grew out of that small, struggling group of 1913). Not only that, but at the time of this writing, there are at least twenty other Assemblies of God churches in the city and in nearby communities.

One block north of Central Assembly stands the International Headquarters of the Assemblies of God, giving leadership to a worldwide constituency of over thirty million believers.

A part of the headquarters structure is Gospel Publishing House, which at the time of this writing was producing an average of over twenty-five tons of literature every day throughout the year.

The training of ministers? In Springfield there are four

Assemblies of God colleges, and their alumni minister around the world: Central Bible College, Evangel College, Assemblies of God Theological Seminary, and Berean College, which provides correspondence courses.

How marvelously God fulfilled the Sizelove vision, doing far more than anyone could have anticipated. To Him be all the glory.

When Broken Glass Wouldn't Cut

Though he was a small boy at the time, the late Bernhard Johnson, a well-known missionary-evangelist to Brazil, never forgot what happened to Sebastian, the town bully. He was a brute of a man—he stood six foot six and weighed 245—who terrorized the townspeople of Alfenas in Brazil. Because of his incredible strength, even the police were afraid of him.

One day by chance he came by a shoe factory that had been converted into a church, where new believers were enjoying a service. Determining to put an end to what he considered a new and false religion, Sebastian stomped up the rickety stairway, striking terror into the heart of the usher who met him and fearfully invited him in.

As the huge figure lumbered down the aisle to the only vacant seat, on the front row, the young pastor was so frightened he hardly knew what to do. For a long time he led them in choruses about the blood of Christ but finally began to preach about the love of God from John 3:16—the only verse he could remember at the moment!

God worked the miracle of salvation for Sebastian that night as he responded to the altar call. His life was changed completely, the news spread throughout the area, and several weeks later when people learned the new convert was to be baptized, thousands came to watch, mainly to ridicule and persecute. The young pastor had invited Bernhard's father, a missionary to Brazil, to administer the baptism.

Only a few knew that some enemies of the gospel had thrown broken bottles into the water at the baptismal site so Sebastian and Bernhard's father would cut their feet and have to leave town in humiliation.

For over half an hour Sebastian testified of his conversion and asked forgiveness for his evil actions of the past. Then, as he and missionary Johnson stepped into the water, God baptized the new believer in the Holy Spirit, and he came out of the water speaking in a heavenly language.

Those who knew about the broken glass plot gasped in amazement, for neither man showed any signs of injury or pain.

One of the persecutors decided something had gone wrong and jumped into the water. Instantly, he began screaming in pain and had to be rushed to the hospital for emergency treatment of his lacerated feet. It proved a miracle had taken place.

Such demonstrations of the power of God have caused the work of God to prosper greatly in Brazil, as well as around the world.

The Miracle Herd

The winter of 1978 had been hard for the Crooked Creek Ranch, owned by Don and Lanoma Hendrickson. First, it was an accident that had necessitated back surgery for Don. After time spent in the hospital, he was back home on the Snake River in Washington being cared for by his wife, a licensed practical nurse. Laid up for several weeks, he could not care for his 185 calves, so his son-in-law Bob Cooper had to carry the full load of the ranch, with the wives helping out as they were able.

Times had been bad, now they got worse. In December some of the calves contracted pneumonia, and by January all 185 were sick. This was serious. If a calf misses even two feedings—for any reason—it takes two weeks to regain the weight it loses. Having this many sick could mean disaster.

Six calves died. The vet confirmed it was pneumonia and treated the entire herd with medication, which was all he could do. One calf was in bad shape; infection had affected its brain. Special medication failed to bring relief, and the calf died. They left its carcass in the barn, for there wasn't time to carry it away.

Several days later twenty-eight calves were penned separately in a barn with little chance of survival. They were wheezing and coughing and bleeding profusely from their noses. The rest of the herd were in feeder lots next to the house. All of them were down coughing and wheezing. It looked bad.

Then God came on the scene. From the Asotin, Washington, Full Gospel Assembly of God, where the Hendricksons and Coopers were members, came Pastor and Mrs. W. L. Papan and two men, Kenn Crabb and Louis Kiele. While the women watched from outside the fence, the three men walked through the feeder lots praying over the entire area and claiming victory for their friends.

As Don viewed the scene and prayed from his bedroom window, he saw the sick cows jump up, throw their tails over their backs, and race to the feeders. It was obviously a miracle. None of those calves showed any more evidence of sickness.

That was not all. The group next went to the twenty-eight calves inside the barn. Standing outside and looking in, they prayed for those critically sick calves.

The next morning there was no more bleeding or wheezing, not even a cough. They were turned into the feed lot with the other calves. They never lost another calf!

A couple of days later, Bob went into the barn and passed by the little calf that had died the week before. He happened to kick its head, and it moved! He immediately gave it food and water by a stomach tube, and within a few days the calf they had thought was dead was up and eating from a manger—all this after going seven days and fourteen feedings without food or water.

It's no wonder Don and Bob called that herd their "miracle calves."

Paul twice refers to the Old Testament provision "Thou shalt not muzzle the ox when he treadeth out the corn," and once asks, "Does God care for oxen?" Yes, He does, and evidently He cares for calves too—and their owners.

A Civil War Miracle

How the story of this miracle came to be known and how the miracle was later verified is almost as fascinating as the story itself.

In the late 1920s, Bert Webb, later a well-known leader in the Assemblies of God, was pioneering a church in Granada, Minnesota. One night word came to him that an elderly Civil War veteran, Colonel Trumble, wanted to see him. The colonel had become acquainted with the young pastor through a small monthly magazine he had produced and circulated in the community.

So traveling about thirty miles out into the countryside, Pastor

Webb came to the bedside of the old soldier. "I'm not going to make it, Preacher," the colonel said, "and I want to tell someone about a miracle I experienced during the Civil War."

In feeble tones the old man told of being one of many Union soldiers incarcerated at the infamous Andersonville, Georgia, prisoner-of-war camp. History has recorded the horrible living conditions that prevailed there; it was almost as bad for the guards as for the prisoners of war. Men died by the hundreds.

Food was scarce, Colonel Trumble recalled, but perhaps even worse was the scarcity of water. The supply was not sufficient to meet their needs. In desperation, he said, one day he and several other prisoners went to the western edge of the encampment and kneeled in prayer.

"We prayed that God would help us," he said. "To our surprise, in a few minutes a huge black cloud came and stood above the stockade. Suddenly, a brilliant flash of lightning burst out from the cloud, striking a huge rock and splitting it apart. A stream began to gush out and continued to flow."

Bert Webb thanked the dying man, prayed with him, and returned home. It was a fascinating story, but he wondered if perhaps it was just a figment of the imagination of a dying soldier, soon to fade away. So for five years he kept the story to himself.

Then came a remarkable development. Bert Webb had resumed his evangelistic ministry and in the spring of 1935 was conducting a revival campaign at the North Highlands Assembly of God in Columbus, Georgia. He had felt led to speak on "The Water of Life." As he was preaching, he suddenly felt impressed to tell the story, which he had kept secret until then.

The results surprised him. The atmosphere in the church seemed to become charged as though with electricity, and many people came to the altar to find Christ.

That was not all. Afterwards, people swarmed around the preacher. "We know about that spring," they said. "The site of Andersonville is just a few miles from here. The story is true."

The next day Bert Webb went with friends to the site of the miracle. There in the center of the former camp was the spring with a stone springhouse covering the rock from which the water issued. And above the door was a sign that read Providence Spring, commemorating the miracle that had produced it.

A fitting title. It was a providential miracle of God that had produced the spring. It was by providence a young preacher had learned of it. And it was providential that he had been inspired to tell the story for the first time at a place where the people could verify it.

God Gave Him a New Stomach

One of the doctors said, "I never believed in miracles before, but I do now!" In fact, it was a series of miracles that kept W. Gene Baker alive for over seven months. The Sunday school director for the Oklahoma district of the Assemblies of God during the 1970s survived one crisis after another during 1977 and 1978, each of which was life threatening.

It began in mid-October 1977. He was rushed to the hospital with what at first seemed to be the flu, but it soon became apparent his problem was much more serious. He was to spend seven months in the hospital, five months of that time in intensive care. He received 160 pints of blood and had six major surgeries.

He says, "I remember very little of those months." One reason was, for over a month and a half he was given a shot of morphine every four hours to relieve the pain. People experienced with the effects of the drug say it is a miracle he did not develop an addiction and had no problem of withdrawal. After the mid-November surgery, six hours long, surgeons told his wife, Doris, he had a bleeding ulcer, and they had removed two-thirds of his stomach.

The surgery did not solve the problem. He needed surgery for three Sundays in a row. In one of them surgeons removed the rest of his stomach. His body was not making any blood, and every few days they had to replenish the supply.

After this fourth surgery, Baker went into a "code blue" shock, and his blood pressure dropped to zero. Mrs. Baker, who had been with him in the intensive care unit, told their four children he had died. However, the doctors put him on a breathing machine, and he recovered.

In December 1977 Baker began hemorrhaging. The doctors did not feel he could stand more surgery, so they left him bleeding. But finally they realized they had no alternative except surgery. They found that infection had severed an artery, so they sewed it up and hoped the wound would heal from the inside out.

Shortly after this grueling experience, Baker was cleared to enter the Veterans Hospital in Oklahoma City. There doctors discovered he had a staph infection and pneumonia. Taking X rays they found his esophagus had become detached and was not functioning. He was scheduled for life-saving surgery.

His wife was attending a service at Lakeside Assembly the evening before the surgery. She felt impressed to request prayer that her husband would receive a new stomach. She knew it was a strange request that might cause ridicule, so she was reluctant and delayed doing so. However, just before Pastor Greg Whitlow dismissed the service, she mustered up her courage and made the request.

Driving home that night, she sang to herself the chorus "Trust and Obey," and put her faith in the Lord.

The next day the doctors at the V.A. Hospital made an exciting discovery. X-ray tests showed something unusual had occurred. Taking Mrs. Baker to a viewing room, a technician showed her that "a new, little stomach had mysteriously formed."

God had intervened supernaturally. Gene Baker completely recovered and continued in his district position another ten years.

Divine Delay

Although Regina Northrop had lost her pastor-husband, Robert, to Hodgkin's Disease in 1972, she took four of her children to the 1975 General Council of the Assemblies of God at Denver, Colorado. Her son, Dary, was leaving from Denver to work on a fishing boat in North Carolina for two weeks, so she drove him and two other ministers to the airport.

They took their luggage out of the car, said their good-byes, and proceeded into the terminal.

Regina got back into the car, started the motor, put the lever into drive, and pressed down on the accelerator to move away. But nothing happened. She pushed down harder—again no response. Regina got out of the car, looked under the pedal, and began to think of getting help.

Praying as she got back in the car, the thought came to Regina, *I wonder if it will work in reverse.* It did, so she put it in drive and slowly it moved forward.

Then she heard someone knock on the car. It was her son, Dary. "Mom," he said, "I left my ticket in the backseat." Regina began to cry as she said, "Son, God just performed a miracle."

The answer to prayer had a threefold benefit. First, it helped the mother out of a difficult situation. Second, Dary would probably have missed his flight if she had been able to drive away sooner. And also, Regina, now Mrs. Milton McCorcle, says she felt God was reassuring her, letting her know He would always provide for her and her children.

An Eccentric's Prayer

Tom Nicholas was a well-loved brother at Faith Tabernacle in Clio, Michigan. He was short of stature but long on love, always willing to help in any way he could. He served as a deacon of the church for many years.

From his earliest days as a child, Tom had suffered from physical ailments. He had asthma and curvature of the spine, which crowded all his vital organs to the left side of his body. From his work in the copper mines of Upper Michigan he also had developed a double hernia. His son Larry wrote about his father's healing in 1955, after he had suffered kidney failure.

The doctor who treated him at the Flint, Michigan, hospital told his wife, Iris, it was surprising he had even reached the age of forty with such physical problems (he was now in his sixties).

After Tom had spent three weeks in the hospital, the doctor took Iris and Larry aside. The doctors (he included himself), he said, had done all they could, but to no avail. So Tom was sent home to die. He suffered greatly as he lay in bed, unable to sit up or roll over. Even a touch on the bed caused severe pain.

About a week after Tom came home from the hospital, God used an unlikely instrument with an unorthodox method to bring healing. A foreign believer, Carl Kvasnica, phoned the Nicholas home and told Iris in his very broken English that God had told him to come over and pray for her husband. Hesitantly, because Carl was somewhat eccentric, Iris agreed.

A half hour later Carl drove up to the house. Getting out of his car with his concertina in hand, he began singing as he made his way to the porch, "There is power, power, wonder working power in the precious blood of the Lamb." Then going up to the porch, he began to rebuke the devil and plead the blood of Christ over every part of the house, from front to back. The family watched with mixed feelings. They appreciated his desire to help, but they weren't used to this kind of procedure.

There was more to come! Carl was praying in other tongues as he entered the room where Tom Nicholas lay helpless on the bed. He paused for a moment and then suddenly leaped up into the air and came down astride the small form of the man on his deathbed. Larry thought his mother would faint.

No sooner had Carl's feet hit the bed than he grabbed Tom's hand and pulled him up, commanding in a loud voice, "In the name of Jesus be healed!"

To the complete surprise and great delight of those present, as Tom Nicholas's head came up off the pillow, his color returned, and he was totally well!

Larry Nicholas reported, "Camp meeting broke out. I can still see Dad walking from one end of that house to the other, tears streaming down his cheeks, hands raised high, worshiping God." The pastor and church friends were called, and the rejoicing continued for several hours.

Tom Nicholas never returned to that sickbed and lived more than twenty-five years longer, passing away four months before his ninetieth birthday.

Well, the Bible records many victories by unlikely instruments and unusual methods. Usually, they were a one-time action, but God honors faith in any form.

(The Nicholases were faithful members in my first pastorate at Clio many years ago.)

A Human Torch Made Whole

The mind of G. W. Hardcastle Jr. was a bitter battleground that Monday morning in July 1949 as he began a day of work for an electrical company in Fort Smith, Arkansas. From his early teens he had felt the call of God to the ministry, but off and on he had rebelled against the idea.

He had thought of various alternatives: God needed laymen such as Christian businessmen who could give their time, tithes, and talents to help a pastor in a local church. So earlier he had enrolled at Texas A & M to study mechanical engineering. It was only about one hundred miles from Houston, where his parents had been pastoring at the time.

But he was miserable, and finally one day he ran from the chemistry building to his dormitory room and wept out his heart before God. He received a feeling of freedom and tranquillity he had never known before. After returning home for the summer, he made plans to attend Bible school.

However, Satan again applied his subtle pressures, and G. W. began doubting his call. On Sunday, July 18, he told his parents and girlfriend he had decided to return to Texas A & M to pursue an engineering career. His parents, now pastoring at Fort Smith, Arkansas, left that night for the Oklahoma District camp meeting in Oklahoma City.

Now, the next morning, G. W. was in a turmoil as he began the day's work of running a cable from a new electric substation to a service pole over a block away where his foreman was stationed.

Around G. W.'s neck was a battery tester with two leads. This would put enough electricity into the dead cable to make the light shine to the foreman's location, enabling him to do his work. The cables were arranged in groups of three, making a circuit, and there were nine circuits where he was to work. He climbed into position and braced himself against a steel beam that led straight to the ground.

When the foreman signaled G. W. to begin, he took hold of a cable. Immediately, more than four thousand volts of electricity shot through him. He had grabbed a live one! The three cables split apart and began to whip about like snakes. Their spitting flames fused together and engulfed him with their high amperage, holding him in a searing, electrifying ball of flame.

G. W. had never known such pain. The force of the blast knocked him backwards, turning him over and leaving him hanging by his right leg. It felt as if it was being burned off, and his entire body felt like wax paper that had been thrown into the fire.

Two men raced to rescue him, letting him down by his belt, for his scorched flesh would have fallen from his body if they had touched it. An ambulance rushed him to a Fort Smith hospital. G. W. realized his parents were over two hundred miles away and asked Dr. Ken Thompson to contact two deacons from his father's church, Charles Fite and Darrel Hon.

Dr. Thompson told the two men G. W. probably would not survive. He said, "He will be unconscious in three hours and will never regain consciousness, unless briefly, before he expires."

Fite hurried to a phone and called the parents. Immediately, one thousand people at the camp meeting went to their knees in prayer on behalf of the young man.

As the parents entered the Fort Smith hospital they met a discouraging prognosis, "If your boy lives, which is unlikely, he will probably have no use of his arms and legs. His ears, nose, and lips will be gone. You wouldn't want this boy to live. He will probably be a basket case the rest of his life. He would be a drawn, distorted mass of flesh, an object of pity."

The father received from God a supernatural gift of faith. "Gentlemen," he said, "not only am I going to pray that my boy will live, but that God will heal him completely."

It was a hideous sight that met the parents as they entered their son's room. His body was burned to a crisp, almost beyond recognition. His head had swollen larger than a basketball. His upper lip was over his nose, and his lower lip was down over his chin. A watery fluid was dripping constantly from his body until he wallowed in it. The blood had changed to a yellowish-white color. He was swathed from head to toe in white Vaseline and wrapped in inch-thick pressure bandages. A needle in each foot fed plasma and whole blood into his veins for sixteen hours at a time.

At midnight on Thursday, three days after the accident, the doctor recommended that G. W.'s parents get some rest, for this was a crisis time. If his temperature should rise one degree, it would be the end, he said. He promised to let them know if there should be a major change.

It was not long before the parents received the phone call they dreaded and hurried back to the hospital. G. W.'s temperature had risen two degrees. The unbearable pain had made him a raging maniac. It took five people to hold him down.

The godly father stepped to his son's bedside, laid his hand on his head and breathed a brief prayer.

Then the miracle happened! Instantly G. W. fell back, his head landing on his pillow, and fell asleep.

"My boy!" his mother cried. "He's dead! He's gone!"

The men in the room helped her to the corridor where she could lie down. Her husband kneeled beside her, saying, "Mother, he's not dead. The Lord just healed him. You've got to believe, Mother."

The young man lay motionless. There was no sign of life. But as dawn broke Friday morning, he awakened. His first words were, "I've had the best night's rest I've ever had."

"Reverend Hardcastle," said the doctor, "it seems the boy is going to live. However, you must remember that we have no idea what he will look like."

While lying there awake, G. W. dedicated his entire life to God. "Lord," he prayed, "if you will heal me completely, I will do anything or go anywhere for you. But, Lord, I can't preach the fullness of your Word from a wheelchair. I won't be accepted with my face scarred, with no features. How can I preach without eyes, ears, nose, lips, legs, and arms?"

Finally the day came for the bandages to be removed. It took several hours. When the doctor saw the patient's face, he could not contain himself. "My God, son," he exclaimed, "this is a miracle!" Thinking that the victim would have no nose, lips, ears, or facial features whatsoever, he said it again, "This is a miracle."

Two and a half months after entering the emergency room, G. W. Hardcastle Jr. walked out of the hospital and drove home. He went on to have a highly effective ministry as an evangelist and pastor, a living testimony to the miracle-working power of God.

A "Mummy" Gets Healed

A "mummy"—that's what close friends called Rose Osha of Washington, Indiana, at the depth of her awful experience. An unusual kind of cancer would begin deep under her skin, rise to the surface, then fester, causing the skin to drop off. This would leave her blood vessels, bones, and the surrounding flesh exposed. No medication helped, and skin grafts were impossible.

Physicians had to use casts on her legs to serve as skin. A toe from each foot had rotted away, and the cancer had eaten the flesh from her chin and face, leaving the cheekbones exposed. On her right temple she had a three-inch hole "blown out when they were draining some infection from my face." She required a two-inch-thick cast from her neck to her hips. She did indeed look like a mummy. Her condition grew worse, and finally one of two doctors who attended her, Dr. Joe, informed her she had only about six months to live.

The doctor's prognosis startled Rose into remembering her Christian upbringing. She had been raised in a Christian environment but during her high school years had turned away from God and lived a fast, sinful life.

Rose's health problems had begun during a 1962 pregnancy, when the doctors lanced what they thought was an infected milk gland. But after the birth of a baby girl (who lived only two hours) a malignancy was discovered. During the pregnancy it had been able to grow at a rapid pace. Though her condition grew worse and worse, Rose still did not turn back to God. In fact, she resented it when people told her they would pray for her. She would tell them, "I have enough problems without your prayers." She did not, however, blame God for her troubles.

The time came when the casts were unable by themselves to hold her body together, so the doctors tried a different procedure. They secured various bones together by stainless steel metal clamps, three inches to eight inches long. There were 739 of them under the casts!

Her blood vessels had begun to deteriorate, hindering the flow of blood. To solve this problem doctors installed 312 plastic tubes, helping the blood to flow from normal areas to places where it was needed.

These were the conditions Rose endured for sixteen years.

Rose had two doctors with her from the inception of the cancer. Dr. Jim, who was a Christian, encouraged her, "Turn your life over to the Lord. He is the only one who can possibly help you." In contrast, Dr. Joe was an atheist. Each time his partner prayed for Rose, he would say, "You're wasting your time, there is no God. We're the only ones who can possibly help her."

There was a period of two years, beginning in 1971, when Rose had to stay in bed because of her weakened condition. Then she struggled out of bed into a wheelchair, advanced to using a walker, and finally walked without any assistance. However, she was in horrible pain around the clock, and finally painkillers had no effect.

A great change occurred when revival services were being conducted at the Assemblies of God church in Washington. Rose Osha waited almost too late, until after the last prayer of the last meeting of the revival, but believers helped her, and she and her husband, "Bud" (Andrew), turned their lives over to God.

The people of the church began praying for Rose's healing, but it was eighteen months before there was any sign of healing, and it came gradually. How God works belongs to His sovereignty. We will understand on the other side. Rose learned later how and why God used eighteen months to complete her healing.

In July 1975 the miraculous healing began. Rose and her husband were driving to a service at an Evansville church when suddenly she felt a pain in her right hand. At first she thought a clamp or tube had broken. That was serious, for there was no way they could be replaced because of the condition of her flesh.

Rose peeked under the bandage covering her arm, and to her amazement, for the first time in sixteen years there was flesh instead of open exposed sores. She began unwrapping her hand and saw what amounted to a completely new hand covered with new flesh.

This extremely fascinating journey of healing, covering eighteen months, was beginning with her right hand. Rose said to Bud, "Where are the tubes and clamps under this new flesh?" They had disappeared. Her husband said, "God must have just dissolved them."

The healing of various parts of Rose's body was gradual, and every time there was a new healing (about every two weeks) Rose had to go back to the hospital for another X ray. Each time, the tubes and clamps had also disappeared.

Surprisingly, Dr. Joe, the atheist, was unimpressed, saying, "It's nice that you are getting better, but there is no God!"

This response came in spite of the fact that he was one of the doctors who had put the tubes and clamps in place at the beginning of her cancer and was the one taking the X rays.

In spite of the series of healings, Rose grew weak and required blood transfusions periodically. But one morning Rose heard an audible voice, "Rose, your temple is healed" (not her face, just the temple). She heard the voice three more times.

Rose had to be sure she was moving in the will of God before she removed the bandages on her face, so she said, "If it's you, Lord, give me a sign." In a couple of seconds the hallway of their trailer home lit up with a brilliant light, and there in the middle stood the Lord with His arms outstretched. He spoke, "Rose, I said the temple is healed."

She raced into the living room to tell Bud the news. There had been a three-inch hole, with no hair, under the bandage. Going into the bathroom, they began removing the bandage. As the last fraction of an inch of the bandage was being uncovered, new flesh was covering the place formerly exposed. Then, before their eyes, hair began to appear. Rose says, "My hair grows fast, but it doesn't grow one-fourth of an inch in thirty seconds."

By the time they could get to the doctor, the rest of her face had been completely healed. And once again, when the X ray was taken, not a tube or clamp could be found.

Another time, on a Sunday morning, Rose was at her sister's

home having a cup of coffee when the cast on her right arm seemed to be loose (it needed to fit tightly to hold the clamps and tubes in place). It became very painful, and she was holding the cast in her left hand when she happened to pull the cast forward. It slid over her hand, and there she sat with a molded cast in her left hand and a brand new right arm. "I have a few scars," Rose says, "but I don't mind them at all."

One day as Rose was putting on her hose, she discovered that sometime during the night the Lord had restored her two missing toes. There are no marks to indicate they are not the toes she received at birth.

The saga of healing continued. In March 1979 Rose thought that for the first time in sixteen years there was flesh under the cast still on her upper torso. The cast weighed seventy-six pounds and had not been removed for several years. Rose phoned Dr. Jim, asking him if the cast could be removed. The doctors warned her that since there was no flesh under the cast, if the air hit her body it would cause sudden death.

Tests showed there was a very thin layer of flesh underneath the cast, and also 251 clamps and 115 plastic tubes. Rose told the doctors to go ahead, that she had placed her faith in the Lord, and He would not fail her.

When they had carefully removed the cast, they found fresh flesh.

An hour later another X ray was needed. The eight people who stood there became witnesses that God had dissolved all the remaining clamps and tubes in her body.

The Christian doctor, Jim, was praising the Lord, but the atheist, Dr. Joe, said, "I don't believe it. There is no place for the tubes and clamps to hide. I'm glad you're better, but God didn't do it."

In some ways, the rest of this story is the best part. Rose was required to go back for a checkup. When she walked into Dr. Joe's office to begin the tests, he said, "Rose, could I have a word with you?"

Not even looking at him, for she was in a hurry, Rose said, "Write me a letter, phone me, or put it on tape, I'm in a hurry," and she went about her tests.

When she came back to his office, the atheistic doctor once more said he wanted to talk with her. As she looked at him, for the first time she saw tears flowing down his cheeks, and he said, "I thought you would have time for a word of prayer."

Rose hurried to get Dr. Jim, and as the three prayed together, Dr. Joe found the Lord and also was baptized in the Holy Spirit.

He said he could no longer doubt the power of God. After seeing clamps and tubes dissolve and flesh appear on a body, he could no longer refrain from wanting God in his life.

Later the newly born-again doctor won several nurses and other doctors to the Lord.

Prayer Dissolved the Fog

The spring night of Tuesday, June 5, 1962, had started out well for the young people on board the Goodtime II. It had been chartered by the Christian Youth Fellowship of the Greater Cleveland area for a three-hour cruise on Lake Erie. The passengers were from two Nazarene churches, two Mennonite churches, one Christian Reformed church, and the Bedford Assembly of God.

Rain had fallen steadily for two days, but no one wanted to cancel the cruise. All were glad when the rain stopped an hour before departure and the sun began to break through the clouds. As the boat pulled away from the East Ninth Street pier, the skies were clear.

The first two hours were very enjoyable, though uneventful. However, about 10:45 P.M., as they were preparing to return to the dock, the boat was asked to give clearance to a large ore freighter leaving the harbor. During the ten-minute wait just outside the breakwater, a thick cloud bank rolled in, producing zero visibility.

The Goodtime dropped anchor and the engines were idled. Though the Coast Guard station was only a short distance away, neither it nor the brilliant harbor lights could be seen through the fog. The growl of the fog horn made the situation more eerie and frightening. Children sensed there was danger. Youth began to chatter and laugh nervously. The faces of older people revealed their own apprehension and anxiety. The pilothouse was buzzing with activity; Skipper John Vitato and his crew were doing all they could to allay fears. Ship-to-shore messages from the radio operator asked the Coast Guard to notify families and employers about the situation.

A radio receiver monitored constant messages from the Coast Guard and the U.S. Weather Bureau. The news was not good.

They reported that the entire harbor was fogbound, with its density increasing.

The midnight hour passed and the outlook was still grim. Children were crying and people were milling about nervously on all three decks. The Mennonite pastors and the Assemblies of God pastor, Fred H. Neubauer, agreed it was high time for someone to take the lead and call the people to prayer. They made their way to the pilothouse and told the skipper their desire. He agreed, and one of the Mennonite pastors took the microphone. He asked all on board to join in serious prayer, then asked Neubauer to lead in prayer.

Neubauer reported, "As I shut my eyes and began to pray, faith brought into focus a likeness of Christ walking toward the boat. He was not coming from above, nor from the side of the fog, but out of it. As He neared the boat in the vision, the fog parted and rolled away to either side. It seemed that Jesus said to me, 'Fear not; I am the Pilot and Master of all.'

"Within five minutes after prayer and singing some timely songs and choruses, a staccato tapping on my arm caused me to look through tear-filled eyes toward the shore. The harbor lights could be seen! The pea-soup fog was thinning out. In another five minutes the entire harbor was clear of fog, and the downtown lights of Cleveland were clearly visible."

Skipper John Vitato asked to speak over the P.A. system. He said, "In all my years of marine experience I have never seen fog move in so quickly and solidly. Believe me, I had my anxious times—if not fears. It has been worth all the agony of these hours to have it proved to us there is a God who answers prayer.

"I can tell you now what I couldn't before prayer: according to the Weather Bureau and the Coast Guard, we should have been here all night, in fact, until daybreak and longer. There is a God! How else could such heavy fog clear away as quickly as it did. We witnessed a miracle tonight!"

Tingling with excitement and with the words of the skipper ringing in their ears, the passengers watched while the crew weighed anchor, the engines speeded up, and they moved under a clear, starlit sky toward the harbor and home.

One-half hour after the last passenger disembarked, the Cleveland harbor became—true to the weather report—completely fogbound until nine-thirty the next morning!

God Was Their Fire Department

"Mommy, will God put out the fire?" three-year-old Billy asked. "I don't know," answered Eva Neckels truthfully, "but we'll ask Him."

It was a hot July evening in 1965, and lightning danced all around the California valley surrounding their home. About to finish washing the supper dishes, Eva looked out of her kitchen window and saw lightning strike and ignite tinder-dry grass a short distance away. A strong wind was blowing the flames toward them.

"Honey," she screamed to her husband, "look—the lightning just started a fire!"

He ran to their landlord's house to call for help on the two-way radio. The nearest neighbor who could provide assistance was three miles away, up the valley.

The mother and child kneeled by the bed and prayed. They told God how vulnerable and alone they felt and asked for His help and protection.

Then they ran outside to see how near the fire was. Unless something happened—and quickly—they would have to run to safety, leaving the home to the flames.

All of a sudden the sky turned black, and almost before they knew it they were soaked by a downpour. It lasted only a few moments, but when they looked toward the fire again, it was out!

A few minutes later the neighbor Eva's husband had called pulled into their driveway. He was astonished at the miracle, for he had seen the rain put out the fire.

That same night lightning strikes kindled other fires nearby, one of which burned for almost a week. But God had extinguished the fire for people who trusted Him.

The family never forgot the time God became their fire department. Eva Neckels is certain it influenced her child to accept Jesus as his Savior at an early age.

A Succession of Miracles

Shari (Ball) Gambino was born to a well-known family of Central Assembly, Springfield, Missouri. Her miracle history began at an early age, for she was born blind, had only one lung, and her internal organs were out of normal position. Fourteen outstanding specialists examined her and declared there was nothing they could do for her. Because she had only one lung, it seemed evident she could not survive an operation.

But her great-grandmother Estes and a friend, Mrs. Hoy, prayed for Shari all night, and when the doctors checked the infant the next morning, she could see, she had two perfect lungs, and internally she was in a normal condition.

In her midtwenties Shari traveled all over the world for five years as the hostess on a corporate jet of the Atlantic Richfield Corporation. However, for several years she had suffered severe backaches, and the pain was increasing rapidly.

A computerized tomography scan revealed a lump in her spine. Her orthopedic surgeon, Dr. Glen Wheeles, had been giving her shots and said she would need back surgery. She also learned she had a degenerative spinal disease and a herniated disk.

Unknown to the doctor, Shari's pain had become so unbearable, she had begun giving herself shots of dimethyl sulfoxide directly into her veins (a drug usually given to horses!). It was extremely difficult to walk and to get up and down. She was nauseous and increasingly spending much time in bed.

Shari's problems were not over. In June 1989 she slipped on a wet floor. As she fell she put her right hand behind her to ease the fall, and the wrist and arm were badly broken. The bones did not heal properly and had to be broken again and set, this time with pins. Her pain continued, and strong medication and morphine could not kill it.

When X rays were taken again, it was discovered that the pins had split the bones. Further surgery became necessary to graft bone from her leg to the arm. A metal plate was added.

After her release from the hospital, Shari went to another doctor who administered daily shots into her neck. They proved of no value, so back to the hospital she went. A tube was inserted in her back to provide a steady flow of medicine.

For Shari, 1989 was a bad year. She became addicted to drugs because of the excessive medication she had taken. Her grandmother, Ogrieda Hall, died in November. By the end of the year Shari had even made an unsuccessful attempt at suicide.

But God was not through with Shari. She was encouraged to enter the Teen Challenge program in Fort Worth, Texas. The program insists on commitment to Jesus Christ as the answer to drugs and has a success rate, for those who follow it, of 86 percent! It worked for Shari. She was there almost a year and won the battle.

Shari began listening to faith-building TV programs and on January 11, 1991, planned to fly to a healing service. But about five-thirty that morning, as she was watching a service, she suddenly sensed the presence of Jesus in her room. She felt totally immersed in His love and began to worship with all her heart. When she had finished, she knew God had healed her.

Shari waited until October of that year before returning to Dr. Wheeles and telling him what had happened. When he examined her, the lump on her back was gone, and her arm was normal. He said, "Shari, this is a miracle."

Shari Gambino is now a licensed massage therapist. Daily it requires hours on her feet and strenuous use of her hands and wrists. She says she chose this work "so I could give something back to the Lord, to testify about what He has done for me."

Sight through a Plastic Eye

Friday night, June 29, 1951, was a memorable evening for seven-year-old Ronald Coyne. Neither he nor anyone else at the revival services of the Assemblies of God church of Sapulpa, Oklahoma, was anticipating what would happen to him.

Daisy Gillock was the evangelist, conducting services for Pastor Lonnie Osborn. As part of her ministry she prayed for those who were sick. Ronald's brother Russell, pastor of the Trinity Bible Congregation, Sun City, California, tells what happened.

Upon the evangelist's invitation, Ronald went forward merely for a sore throat. But the evangelist noticed that one of Ronald's eyes did not look right and asked him about it. He replied, "I'm blind in one eye."

Nine months earlier it had been necessary to remove Ronald's right eye, and he had been fitted with an artificial one.

Evangelist Gillock prayed a simple prayer that God would give him sight, and instantly the miracle occurred.

For over forty years, until his death in early 1994, Ronald Coyne traveled all over the world demonstrating this remarkable miracle, even appearing on such TV programs as *Phil Donahue* and *That's Incredible*.

Cake Supply Increased

It was their first term (1973–1977) in Costa Rica, and missionaries Gerald and Carol Robeson had been conducting services every night for ten months. They planned a joyous occasion for new believers in their crusade church at Moravia, a suburb of San Jose. That Christmas Eve many new converts would be celebrating their first Christmas as Christians. The church was presenting special music, filmstrips of the Christmas story, and refreshments.

The women of the church had baked mountains of cake, and Carol had borrowed all the electric coffeemakers she could locate among her friends.

It was a wonderful time of singing Christmas carols. At the halfway point in the service, the women served cake and coffee to everyone.

As the women were cleaning up after the service, they discovered ten sheet cakes were left over. Carol suggested they serve the remainder at the New Year's Eve service the next week. She figured that if they froze what was left and cut the pieces in half, they would have enough for about four hundred people.

It was a gargantuan task to load into their compact car ten sheets of cakes on plywood, their equipment, and six people; but they made it and somehow stored the leftover cake in neighbors' refrigerator freezing compartments.

So all was in readiness for the New Year's Eve occasion. But as Carol walked through the front door of the church that night, one of the girls met her and said, "We already have over five hundred people here. Are you sure we will have enough cake?"

Carol Robeson could well have sympathized with Martha of Bible times that night. Looking at the crowd, she said hopefully, "I think if we cut some of the bigger pieces of cake twice, we'll make it."

The women counted the pieces of cake and the people who kept coming. Just before serving time they counted one more time: There were 150 more people than pieces of cake!

"What are we going to do, Sister Robeson," the women wailed. "Everyone will take at least one piece of cake, and we don't have enough for everyone."

Silently Carol Robeson sent up an S.O.S., *Lord, You know most of these new converts had to walk a long way to be here for their first New Year's Eve service as Christians. They've come to hear*

Your Word and worship You just as the people followed You into a desert place when You were here on earth, and You fed them. Your Word says You are 'the same yesterday, today, and forever.' So I'm coming to You now because we have a big problem!

She turned to the women who were helping her and asked, "Do you believe the Lord can multiply these cakes as He did when He fed the five thousand with five loaves and two fishes?"

Heads began nodding in agreement, and they joined hands and asked the Lord to perform a miracle. Then the young women picked up the trays of cake and left to serve the large crowd of new believers.

Time after time the workers returned for more cake; and as they finished serving the people, many of them came back with tears streaming down their faces. Not only had every person been served one piece of cake, but many had taken two, and there was cake left over.

Like the servants who saw Jesus turn the water into wine, the workers that night saw what was happening. The next night the whole congregation was told. God is not capricious with His miracles; He always has a purpose. For a young church, witnessing a miracle like this was a wonderful start for their life of faith.

When God Healed an Auto

It was almost a hopeless situation for the three students from Southwestern Assemblies of God College in Waxahachie, Texas.

To save money on a Christmas vacation trip home, David Watson, a freshman at the time, and two young women had decided to drive home together and share expenses. Although the car belonged to one of the women, David was expected to drive (being the male).

The automobile was of ancient vintage and clanked and clattered from the moment they started down the highway. At least there was no fear they would exceed the speed limit, for forty-five miles per hour was the best the car could do. It jerked and missed constantly.

They left about five o'clock on a Saturday afternoon and had driven about an hour when they came to a small town. David slowed as they drove through, then tried to resume speed as they were leaving. But with a loud clank and clatter the engine announced otherwise, then quit altogether.

Fortunately they were able to coast into a nearby service station. Having heard the noise, an attendant came out to check on the problem. His report was not good. Oil was pouring out of a hole in the engine from which a rod was protruding.

"Can you fix it?" the naive young people asked.

"Oh, no!" he replied. "You're going to need a new engine block. I have a friend who might get one for you in the morning. It looks like you're stuck for the night and probably the whole weekend."

The young people looked at each other and laughed anxiously. Their finances totaled less than twenty-five dollars.

David walked around to the front of the car and raised the hood; the girls followed him. Oil was splattered everywhere. They could tell the situation was hopeless.

One of the girls spoke up, "What we need is a miracle!"

"Okay," David said, "let's pray that God will heal this engine." In their simple faith they decided they needed to anoint the motor. They didn't have to look for oil; it was all over the engine. Each young person stuck a finger into the oil and applied some to the breather cap.

David says, "You should have seen the look on the face of the attendant as we prayed. Several men inside the station began laughing."

After the group finished their prayer, they got back in the car and the driver switched on the ignition. To their delight—and the amazement of the men standing around—the engine roared to life without a single clank or clatter. They sped off on their journey, matched the speed limit for the next three hours, and arrived in front of the church where their parents were to meet them.

As they approached the parking lot of the church, there was an awful sound from the engine as it expired. It had to be towed away.

Unusual, but it must have been a great encouragement to the faith of these young people as they completed their training and began their full-time ministry for God. David Watson and his family have had a God-blessed ministry for many years. His faith had a good start.

Instant Healing of Body and Mind

When Charles Crabtree, assistant general superintendent of

85

the Assemblies of God, was a small boy, he witnessed a deliverance that must be labeled as incredible. It happened in 1945, in the living room of the family home in Bangor, Maine.

Daphine Cory, a beautiful young woman from Aroostock County, Maine, had been committed to the state mental institution with a mysterious illness. It had affected her mind and nervous system, causing paralysis from the waist down.

Although the young woman was in such a critical condition that she needed medical attention around the clock, God had put it on the heart of Charles's mother to bring Daphine to their home. Because of Mrs. Crabtree's persistence, she was permitted to do so for a period of three days. A nurse was brought in to help.

On the third morning, the nurse (Mrs. Russell), Mrs. Crabtree, and a daughter, now Hazel Hoskins, were having family devotions. Young Charles was also present. Daphine had been brought in and seated on a low sofa to provide a change of position.

In the middle of the prayer time, Mrs. Crabtree felt impressed to go over to Daphine and pray for her. When she laid her hand on Daphine, the others witnessed a mighty demonstration of the power of God. The young woman was raised to her feet with no human help. She stood in amazement as though she had awakened from a bad dream and began dancing around the living room.

Shortly, the father came home with a bag of groceries, and Daphine was so thrilled at what God had done for her that she ran down the stairs and hugged him—and the contents of the bag flew everywhere.

Daphine was completely cured. Later she married, had a number of children, and served as pianist for the church for many years.

Leg Lengthened for a Future Miss America

In its June 1980 issue, *Christian Life* magazine related the thrilling story of how Cheryl Prewitt's leg was lengthened two inches in answer to prayer. Later, she became Miss Arkansas and then Miss America.

When Cheryl was eleven years old, she and three other family members were badly injured in an automobile accident. Her father reported that when he pulled her out of the backseat of the car, her left leg lay like a cloth over his arm. It was completely crushed above the knee.

She suffered other injuries: her back was cracked, and her face was so badly cut it required more than one hundred stitches. The doctor said she would probably never walk again, and she spent eight months in a cast and in a wheelchair.

Cheryl appeared to be anything but a future Miss America, but the family members were praying people. One day as they were reviewing a series of X rays, they noticed a cocoon of calcium forming around the tiny pieces of bone that were left.

They were thankful to God for His help. Cheryl was able to walk.

However, since Cheryl was so young while her left leg was in the cast, it did not grow as fast as the right leg, so when the cast was removed, the left leg was shorter by almost two inches.

Cheryl was so glad to have two legs she did not complain about the infirmity. At seventeen, during her regular checkup, the doctor told her of an added complication. "Your hips are out of line," he said. "It will probably be hard for you ever to have a family of your own."

The young teenager's Christian faith was strong. She put her faith in the Word of God. Mark 11:23–24 became especially real to her. It speaks of faith moving mountains, and her "mountain" was the short leg. The Scripture passage gives a condition: "whosoever shall not doubt." So she began to affirm her faith, "I will not have this short leg," and to praise God for the answer.

Cheryl heard of a meeting in Jackson, Mississippi, where there would be prayer for the sick. She went with five friends. But before going, the Word of God had been reinforcing her faith so much that at school the day of the trip, she sat down in the hall and pushed her hips against the wall so everybody could see how short her left leg was. She expected to return the next day with a fully grown leg.

She did not even know what the minister preached that night, but when the invitation came for those who sought healing to come forward, Cheryl was one of the first.

"Jesus is the answer," the minister said, and the teenager focused her thoughts on the Lord. When the speaker called people forward he said, "Jesus wore a stripe on His back for your infirmity, whatever it is," and Cheryl said to herself, *If Jesus did that for me, then now's the time to receive this.*

When the minister laid his hands upon Cheryl, she was slain in the Spirit (an experience she had known nothing about) and became oblivious to everything around her. She was overwhelmed with a sense of Jesus' presence and love.

When Cheryl came back to her physical senses, she looked down and watched her left leg grow out to equal the length of her right leg!

Cheryl Prewitt went on to many accomplishments: She was chosen Miss America for 1980, five years after her healing; she received college honors at Mississippi State; she composed many gospel songs; but even more important to her, it appears, is the development of her love relationship with the One who is her Savior, Baptizer in the Holy Spirit, as well as her Healer.

Poison Enough to Kill Ten Men

George Roy Wood, pioneer missionary to China and Tibet, believed he was about to die. He tried to break the crystal on his watch and bend the hands so his wife, Elizabeth, would know the time of his death, but he was too weak to do even that. He told the two Chinese Christians with him that when he died they should take his body, drape it over his horse, and take it back to his wife in Huangyuan, rather than leave it for the vultures.

George's son, George O. Wood, general secretary for the Assemblies of God, says that his father had decided he knew the cause of his illness. It was late 1934, and he was returning from the lamasery (monastery of Lamaist monks) of Hsiang Hsien Si. With two Chinese evangelists he had traveled by horseback to this area where the gospel had not previously penetrated.

He had presented a letter of introduction from the head of another lamasery and asked to see the "living buddha" of the place (the one in charge). A man dressed in a priest's garb met him and said the buddha was not there.

Missionary Wood told the priest he had a gift for all the priests (a printed Gospel portion). The priest replied that he was the first white man they had ever seen and were afraid of him, but he should wait for an answer.

Following Tibetan custom, they served Wood a dish called *tsamba*. They dropped fresh yak butter into his wooden bowl, then piping hot tea was added. (The missionary noted they considered him an ordinary guest, not an honored one, or they would have given him rancid butter.) Wood blew back the butter, drank the tea, and barley flour was poured over the remainder. (It tastes like eating sand.)

The Tibetan priest complimented the missionary on his knowledge of the language and the Tibetan custom of *tsamba* and said, "I'll get people, and you can take pictures and give them your presents."

In his eagerness to distribute the gospel literature, George Wood had failed to notice there had been no exchange of scarves, a traditional Tibetan hospitality gesture that guaranteed safety. He had, however, observed that this man had showed he was not just a priest but actually the buddha of the place by the way he called the people together.

Sensing danger, Wood's companions urged him to leave as soon as possible. Mounting their horses they traveled in the fading daylight to a place called Tsa Pu. By this time the missionary's sickness had become severe. The other men prayed for him, but his condition worsened.

Convinced he was about to die, George Wood prayed, "Lord, I can't pray anymore. My helpers can't pray anymore. Lay it on someone's heart to pray for me." Very soon he began to throw up a dreadful green bile and felt much relieved.

When Wood arrived home in Huangyuan, his wife asked him about the trip, especially if he had met any bandits—a constant danger at that time. When he answered no, she said, "I want to show you something."

She produced some notes she had made one evening. After retiring she had been awakened by a voice saying, *I want you to pray.*

She arose, stirred up the fire for warmth, settled down and said, "All right, Lord, what do you want me to pray about?"

The inner voice answered, *Your husband is sick and dying. He needs prayer.*

Mrs. Wood interceded for a time until she felt God had answered and returned to her bed.

When the wife and husband compared notes as to the days and hours, they learned that her time of intercession corresponded exactly to the night he had been poisoned.

The extent of the miracle deliverance became apparent some time later. George Wood was visiting another Tibetan lamasery, Kum Bom, when some Tibetans came to him and said, "We thought you were dead." They were from the lamasery where he had eaten the poisoned meal.

Evidently they reported Wood's survival, for a delegation came to him from the buddha who had written the original letter of introduction, confessing and apologizing, "They gave you enough poison to kill ten men. Your God is greater than our god. Please come and tell us about Him." Also he received a lifetime passport of safe conduct in their country.

Thirty-nine years later, while George Wood was going through stomach surgery, the Jewish surgeon with over thirty years of gastroenterological practice in Beverly Hills, California, removed a large number of polyps; none were cancerous. He said to his patient, "I've never seen a stomach like this. Normally if there are more than three to five polyps, there is cancer." He asked, "Was there ever a time when your stomach had a shock to its system?"

Telling the story of the miracle left a profound impression on the surgeon.

Once again Jesus' prophecy of Mark 16:18 had been proved true: "If they [believers proclaiming the gospel] drink any deadly thing, it shall not hurt them."

A Dream, a Vision, a Miracle

Grace Sfortunato stood at the nursery window of a Springfield, Missouri, hospital in early 1994, viewing her new grandson. As she did so her mind raced back thirty-three years to the healing of the baby's father when he himself was an infant.

She and her husband were grateful for their thirteen-year-old daughter and their nine-year-old son but they had been asking God for another child.

One evening during devotions, they repeated their request. That night Grace dreamed of a curly-headed boy about a year old sitting in a high chair between her and her husband. Bubbling with joy, she told her husband in the morning and believed it was God's way of telling her He would answer their prayer.

Grace was not surprised later when she learned she was two months pregnant. Though she had experienced some difficulties over the next few months, the day she left for the hospital the Lord assured her He would be with her.

The mother was somewhat perturbed five hours after the baby

boy's birth when she was not allowed to see him, and wondered if he was normal. It was another six hours before he was brought to her bed for a brief glance. The nurse had also turned the room lights low to keep Grace from seeing that the baby was turning blue.

It was not till morning that the mother learned of the baby's shocking condition. He had been born with all his vital organs, except the large bowel, in his chest cavity. His heart was on the right side, and both lungs had collapsed. Chances of survival were about one in a million. The baby had been rushed to the LeBonheur Children's Hospital in Memphis for surgery.

Prior to the doctor's report, the father, Ted, who had stayed all night, went to the cafeteria. While he was gone from the room, suddenly the head nurse stormed in asking for "Brother Ted." Seeing he was not there, she ran from the room, only saying hurriedly, "It's nothing, just an emergency call."

Understandably worried, although she had not yet learned about the baby's condition, Grace leaned back on her pillow.

As she did so, a vision appeared to her: a woman dressed in black and wearing a black veil was holding a baby in her arms. A small coffin was present. A large, ugly man approached the woman, took the child, and was about to place the child in the coffin. At that moment someone (Grace knew it was Jesus) stepped forward, took the baby, and gave it back to the woman.

Immediately Grace knew God was going to spare their child, even though she had not yet been informed that anything was wrong.

A little later, Ted and the doctor came to the room. Both wore pained expressions as the husband asked the doctor to explain the situation. Ted had already signed a release for surgery.

Grace had received such a gift of peace that she did not show much concern, and the doctor doubted she realized the seriousness of the surgery. In faith, Grace assured Ted the baby would survive. Shaking his head doubtfully, the doctor told her not to build her hopes too high.

A dedicated staff of doctors and nurses were in charge of the extensive surgery. After four days of intensive care and three days in a special-care nursery, the baby was released from the hospital. An account of the event was written up in medical records under the heading "The Miracle Baby."

Thirteen months later, Grace's earlier dream was realized at a breakfast table as the parents' curly-haired son, Ted Jr., sat with them in his high chair. And in April 1994, Ted Jr.'s third child, Theodore III, was dedicated to the Lord at Central Assembly. The name is prophetic, for Theodore means "gift of God."

Better Than a Transfusion

"Your wife is in a coma and will die soon," the doctors told Alfonso Quintana. Missionary Bruce Ridpath reported that Eli, the wife of their Colombian friend Alfonso, had been in the hospital more than six months. A midwife had miscalculated the period of her pregnancy, and labor had been induced two months early. Twins had been delivered stillborn, Eli had lost much blood, resulting in further complications, and she had lapsed into a coma.

As the weeks passed, Eli became more and more unresponsive, and now the doctors were saying she was brain-dead.

Alfonso was devastated. "The day I received this news," he said, "I looked at my wife lying in that hospital bed, I.V.'s running everywhere in her body. She looked like a skeleton. I had no hope." He went home crazed with worry and fatigue.

A knock came at the door. It was Eli's cousin William, inquiring about her condition. After Alfonso told him of the doctors' latest report, William asked, "Do you want your wife's health restored?"

Of course he did.

"Then you must commit your life to Jesus Christ, repent of your sins, and thank God for Eli's total healing."

William took Alfonso to a local pastor where he accepted Christ as Savior. Then, as they prayed for Eli's healing, the Holy Spirit revealed that a blood condition was the cause of her illness. So the pastor prayed, "Lord, change her blood completely."

In faith, the pastor told Alfonso, "Bring Eli to church Sunday to testify of her healing."

With peace in his heart, Alfonso returned to the hospital. As he entered Eli's room, he was astonished to see her—all the tubes removed—brushing her hair.

"I thought I was dreaming," Alfonso reported later. "Earlier in the day she had looked like death itself. Now she was awake, brushing her hair, and full of life."

Eli gave her version, "I woke up suddenly and had no idea

what I was doing in a hospital. I felt fine and knew I didn't need all those tubes, so I pulled them out."

Amazed and unable to explain what had happened, the doctors released Eli from the hospital. Alfonso and Eli attended the local church the next Sunday and testified of God's healing power. Many were saved and healed, and Eli herself committed her life to the Lord.

The miracle story was not finished. Doctors had warned Eli that she should never get pregnant again, or she would die. However, within a year she was pregnant once more. When the doctors made the initial examinations and tests, they were baffled. In fact, they repeated the blood tests three times. Shaking their heads, they said, "We're not sure why. We've checked and rechecked—and it makes no sense. Your previous records show your blood type is O-negative, but all our recent tests show you to be O-positive."

Alfonso and Eli are now pastoring a growing church in a poor area of Cartagena, Colombia. Alfonso testifies, "Thank God that the blood of Jesus is powerful enough to change lives—and even someone's blood type!"

Prayer Rescued Him from Death

Billy Burr, missionary to Africa, was trapped in a sea of people, some even calling for his death. The pressure of the bodies was so great that he did not have to hold on to his briefcase. His situation was critical. What a day to die—on December 27, 1979—the eighteenth wedding anniversary for him and his wife, Sue.

On Christmas Day the government had suddenly announced that new currency had been printed, and people had three days to exchange the old money before it became worthless. They could exchange only the equivalent of one thousand dollars, the amount of missions money in the Burrs' possession.

Billy went to the bank on December 26, but the seething crowds made it impossible to reach the bank. So he went at four-thirty in the morning the next day and was near the front of the crowd. He met six young Africans who agreed with him that they would protect each other from the people who might try to get ahead of them.

To their dismay, however, the banker decided to open a side door, and tremendous shoving and pushing ensued. After standing in the hot sun for hours, women began to scream that they were dying. When that availed nothing, they began to scream, "The white man is dying!" Billy, taller than most Africans, knew he stood out in the crowd, and they were speaking of him. They would do anything to get attention.

Suddenly, to Billy's surprise, one of the young men who had made the pact with him earlier yelled, "Let him die!" When the missionary remonstrated, the black man replied that if all the Africans died there, no one would learn of their suffering, but if one American were to die, the story would be printed, and the whole world would know how they were suffering.

Billy Burr knew that many in the crowd felt the same way, and he feared he would not get away alive. How desperate the situation was, Billy would learn later—how the police used tear gas and fire extinguishers to control the crowd. Some were blinded by the white powder of the extinguisher; others were killed in their panic to get inside the bank; still others committed suicide as they lost family fortunes.

God sent deliverance. A national pastor saw Billy's situation, got some military friends, and brought them to the edge of the crowd. "Do you see that white man?" he asked. "He is not a merchant. He is not here to make money off our people. He is one of our pastors. Please help him."

The military men responded. Making a human chain, they fought their way into the crowd and dragged Billy to safety. He was so dehydrated and exhausted he had to sit on his briefcase to regain some strength. The soldiers gave him a military escort into the bank, and he was able to exchange his missions funds.

Now comes the most amazing part of this story. A month after Burr's rescue, a letter came from Maxine Sowers, a prayer partner in Minnesota. She asked what happened on December 27. Early that morning God had awakened her with a heavy burden of prayer for him; she sensed his life was in danger.

In April Billy attended a prayer conference in Lome, Togo. As he entered the hotel lobby, he met a fellow missionary, Paula Flower, who works in Dakar, Senegal. She said, "Before I even ask about Sue and the children, I have to know what happened to you on December 27. I felt your life was in danger. I was busy all day, but I prayed for you all day long."

When Billy came back home, he told his office manager, Kumbali Paul, a former chief who had been marvelously saved, about the two incidents. Kumbali replied, "On December 27, God awakened me very early in the morning. I was startled by a dream I had. I saw your friends preparing for your funeral. I even saw your body in the casket. I was so troubled I ran to the church and rang the church bell (an old tire rim hanging in a tree). People ran to learn about the emergency. I told them they must pray for your safety. We all fell on our knees and began to intercede. After some time the Lord let me see you up walking around. I knew you would be fine."

God had inspired the intercessory prayer of three people on Billy Burr's behalf.

God Uprooted Her Cancer

Ruth and Jerry Bray were perplexed. Seven months earlier they felt God had called them to begin an evangelistic ministry after over fifteen years of a happy pastorate at the Atlanta, Georgia, Assembly of God Tabernacle. And now, in March 1992, she had been diagnosed as having inflammatory carcinoma of the breast. The doctor told them they should cancel their meetings for six months and that she should begin radiation and chemotherapy treatments immediately, followed by a radical mastectomy, then more radiation and chemotherapy.

It was hard to understand why God would allow this to happen. For a second opinion they went to Dr. Martin York, one of the top oncologists in Atlanta, at the Emory University Hospital. He confirmed the prognosis. Ruth asked what her chances would be with the treatments.

He replied, "Frankly, Mrs. Bray, if you take the treatments we can give you a 40 percent chance of cure, but without the treatment your chances are zero."

Ruth responded, "But God can give me 100 percent chance for cure. I will have to pray and talk with my family."

Dr. York said, "Remember, Mrs. Bray, we must get started very soon because of the type of cancer. We don't have time to play with."

Ruth Bray spent much time in prayer. For years she had prayed, "Lord, I want to see miracles come back to the church. Whatever it takes, please bring them back." She little knew her body would become a battleground to determine the sincerity of her prayer.

The tumor began to grow. Determined to do her part Ruth

searched the Scriptures for all the promises about healing. She was reminded of the statement in Matthew 5:23–24 that if a person has anything against us we should initiate reconciliation by going to that individual. She "went" to several by letter, and felt she could now claim the promises in God's Word for herself.

Something unusual happened which encouraged Ruth's faith. One evening, while praying before leaving home, Ruth felt something flip-flop in her breast. It seemed to her that God was cutting the tumor at the root. However, the pain became more intense, and the devil tormented her.

While they were in meetings with Pastor Bruce and Michelle Klepp in Miami, Florida, they were asked to counsel a young woman from Trinidad. After doing so, they joined hands to pray. In the middle of the prayer Michelle stopped them, saying, "Sister Bray, this is for you: Matthew 15:13, 'And whatsoever the Father has not planted, the same shall be uprooted.' "

In early 1993 Ruth Bray testified at Suncoast Cathedral about what God was doing for her. Dr. Ralph Johnson, an oncologist at Bay Front Medical Center, was in the service and came to her to ask some questions, then asked her to come to his office. When she did so, an examination showed there was no sign of inflammatory carcinoma, though the tumor was still present. Three weeks later another examination showed it had decreased in size from a small grapefruit to an orange.

The testing of Ruth's faith was not over; in fact, it became more severe. In May 1993, after ten hours of pain, it was thought she had a kidney stone attack. In surgery to remove the stones, they could not reach the kidney because of a blockage, so she was sent back to Dr. York. His examination revealed the cancer had spread to her ureter, spine, two ribs, and was now in her blood—though the inflammatory carcinoma was gone.

By summer of 1993 Ruth was feeling very weak but continued helping her husband in revival meetings for weeks at a time. Then during a revival meeting in Kansas she prayed, "Lord, I've got to have new strength. I can't continue like this." The next night, when she had finished playing during the altar service, she said to Jerry, "Something has happened, I feel different."

In October 1993 Ruth Bray returned to see Dr. York at Emory University. They took blood tests, after which he came to her and asked how she felt.

"I feel great," she answered.

Dr. York said, "Well, Mrs. Bray, the blood tests show your red and white blood cells and platelets are normal—and, Mrs. Bray, the tumor has detached itself from the chest wall." The promise of Matthew 15:13 had been fulfilled. The cancer had been uprooted.

When she called a week later to get the rest of the lab report, the nurse said, "These tests were to show the functions of the bone, liver, kidneys, and the blood, and they are all normal."

New Flesh for an Old Wound

Missionaries Steve and Charline Norman had arranged a Good News Crusade at La Coruna on the north coast of Spain. Eugenio and Raimundo Jimenez from Latin America were speaking each night. A healing ministry was part of the services.

Since their curiosity was aroused by the newspaper advertisement "Prayer for the Sick," some medical students attended the meetings. They were from the prestigious university located in nearby Santiago de Compostela.

At the end of one of the services, Raimundo Jimenez urged those who had been prayed for to try to do something they had not previously been able to do. One of the students, a young woman, decided to respond. She had sustained a large wound on her leg, and over a period of months, though doctors had applied many stitches, it refused to heal.

To the young woman's surprise, as she cautiously bent her knee, the bandaged wound did not hurt anymore. Encouraged, she went outside and began to run around the pavilion, something impossible before. She was sure then that God had healed her.

Joyfully she joined the other students for supper at a nearby cafe. Filled with enthusiasm, she announced, "I'm going to remove my bandage."

One of the students told Steve Norman later that he groaned within himself, thinking, *Here we are about to eat, and now we have to look at this.*

But revulsion changed to amazement as the group of students witnessed brand new flesh where the open wound had been.

Nine years later the pastor at La Coruna, Manuel Fernandez Vila, informed Steve and Charline Norman, "Because of the fervor of these university students, seven new churches have been started."

Drowned Nine Hours—and Alive!

Jesus raised to life three people: the daughter of Jairus, the son of the widow of Nain, and Lazarus of Bethany. The Book of Acts also records similar miracles. The present-day restoration to life of a young believer on one of the islands of Fiji reminds us of that power of God described in Acts.

The Fijian witch doctors were dancing in glee. They hated seventeen-year-old Isaiah and wanted him dead. A recent convert, Isaiah had become a powerful witness for the gospel and had won many people to Jesus Christ. The witch doctors had been losing their power. Now they were happy because he was lying lifeless on the shore of Vanua Levu, the second largest of the islands of Fiji.

They thought they had won, but they were wrong.

About five-thirty on a June morning in 1978, Isaiah and his pastor, Joe Tilly, had gone fishing at a reef about three and a half miles out in the Pacific Ocean. They reached their destination about seven-thirty, and Isaiah, with a speargun, dived in looking for some of the huge turtles that live in that region.

A turtle of about eighteen inches wide acted strangely: instead of fleeing as they usually do, it circled Isaiah as though about to attack him. It followed both him and his pastor as they went to another reef.

The water was clear, and seeing the turtle, the young diver went after his prey with his speargun. The spear seemed to go through the turtle's neck and lodge in a rock. Isaiah surfaced to get his breath then dived in again to bring back his trophy.

What happened next is not quite clear. Isaiah only remembered touching one of the turtle's flippers and losing consciousness.

When Isaiah did not return, Pastor Tilly went searching for him. The tide had been coming in for about two and a half hours, so the water was much deeper. He saw the speargun lying on the coral and something shiny on the ground—Isaiah's goggles.

Joe Tilly kept trying to retrieve Isaiah's body, but the water was too deep. High tide coming in at 11:00 A.M. forced him to get in the boat and wait until 3:00 P.M. for low tide in order to try again.

Praying for strength, the pastor finally brought the young man's body to the surface, but when he tried to put it in the boat, the craft turned over and sank. He managed to swim with the body to the shore three and a half miles away, getting there about 5:00 P.M., nine hours after Isaiah had drowned.

Many people from nearby villages came to view the body, and the witch doctors chortled with glee.

After his recovery, Isaiah told of what happened to him. Evidently his soul had left his body. He saw himself going up a big highway with flowers on either side. He heard beautiful music and saw a brightly lit village ahead. Many people were in front and behind him, urging him on.

A small person spoke to him, "Someone's calling your name. Maybe he wants something." So Isaiah turned back and soon heard his pastor calling his name and saw his body—swollen and stiff—lying on the beach; many people were there crying.

Isaiah watched for about three minutes while Pastor Tilly prayed. He heard him say, "Wake up, wake up!"

At first, the pastor says, there was no sign of life, but in a few seconds, Isaiah's hands and feet began moving. Then his chest began to heave rapidly, and the pastor could see his young friend was breathing again.

Isaiah remembers opening his eyes and seeing the weeping people and his pastor kneeling over him. He said, "Why did you pray for me?" He had not wanted to come back.

Pastor Tilly answered, "God healed you because He has a purpose for your life."

As Isaiah was raised to his feet, he felt terrible pain all over his body and began to vomit blood and black fluid. They took him to a speedboat, which had been sent for him, and he was taken to the Labasa hospital.

The doctor who made an X ray of Isaiah's lungs said, "I don't know how this could happen. There was salt water in your lungs, but now they are working. I just don't understand it. Lungs are made for air."

The doctors told Pastor Tilly, in the presence of others, that a person lying so long on the ocean floor with his lungs full of sea water could not possibly survive. If such a person should live, his mind would be affected.

Don Henderson, retired professor from Central Bible College, Springfield, Missouri, received this report from Isaiah himself and others in the church at Labasa. He states that Isaiah is still alive and an excellent student and pastor. He has established several churches and is a devoted husband and father.

Healing Cured His Skepticism

"The Blind See, the Deaf Hear, the Lame Walk, Signs, Wonders, and Miracles" proclaimed the large sign. When Gene Mullenax first saw it on a tent at the Arkansas State Fairgrounds that summer of 1958, he did not believe it. How could it be? But Gene was desperate. Though he was only in his midtwenties, most of the time he was bedridden; he hemorrhaged at the smallest exertion, and he was thirty pounds underweight.

He had a wife and two children but was unable to work, so their financial situation was critical.

At first doctors had told him he had a bad case of tuberculosis and sent him to a sanitorium for six weeks of tests. However, the tests proved negative. Next a chest surgeon in Little Rock performed an exploratory operation. He removed three ribs, the right lung, and left a large, ugly hole in his back for drainage of a cyst, which extended through his remaining lung.

He also was left with a drooping shoulder.

Mullenax says, "For the first week after the operation, the doctor didn't know whether I would live or die. I stayed in the hospital for two weeks, then was sent home to spend most of the next six months in bed." He had tried unsuccessfully to resume his work as a sheet metal worker—the continual bleeding hindered him.

So when he saw the huge tent with its bold sign, Gene began to wonder, *Is it possible I could be healed?* He decided to investigate and talked with the controversial evangelist who was holding services in the tent, A. A. Allen. Allen encouraged his young inquirer to believe God, but Gene was still skeptical.

His wife remembers his suspicions. "All day long for several days I would hear, 'Nancy, I don't think that's real. If it's not, I'm going to expose the man to the whole congregation.' He was frustrated and desperate."

However, since there was nothing to lose, Gene decided to go to the meeting and ask for prayer. While waiting in line, he saw in front of him a man holding a baby that had on its lip an ugly growth about the size of a dime.

Gene decided that if the baby was healed, then he would believe for himself. *No one can con a baby into acting out a healing,* he felt.

He was standing less than a foot from the baby's head when Allen prayed for the child. He did not even lay his hands on it.

"That growth disappeared before my eyes the moment he prayed for the baby in the name of Jesus. After that I decided it must be real and that I would believe."

When Gene's turn came, Allen told the audience the problem and asked them to stretch their hands out toward Gene Mullenax in prayer. Then telling him to raise his hands, Allen shouted, "Oh, God!"

Immediately the supernatural power of God touched Gene. "It felt like someone in back of me poured something very warm all over me," he remembers. "I turned around to see who did it, but no one was there. Then it felt like someone stuck a rubber hose in my mouth and just blew me up."

He was instantly and completely healed. His right lung and the three ribs were restored, the drainage hole in his back disappeared, and his shoulder became straight.

On Monday of the next week, Gene went back to work and rapidly regained his normal weight and strength. Over a period of several months, the surgeon who had operated on him took eight X rays of his chest to substantiate the healing.

His story appeared not only in Allen's publication, but later it would be featured on the *Donahue Show*, *CBN*, and the *PTL Club*. In fact, it was scrutinized by the FBI as well: When Allen was suspected of fraudulent practices, agents approached Gene about his healing. After he authorized the release of his medical records to them, he said, "That's the last I saw of them." Gene Mullenax himself went on to be a successful contractor installing sheet metal in large buildings across Arkansas, Louisiana, and Mississippi.

Dead for Thirty-Five Minutes

The future looked sad for Dee McGeough's family. The medical team at a Fort Worth, Texas, hospital was preparing them for what they were sure would happen. The neurologist told Dee's husband, Jack, she was in a coma, and based on what he could determine from the tests they had given, she would remain in one for a week or even more, up to three weeks.

He warned the family not to expect very much. Since she had been "dead" for thirty-five minutes, she might never see, hear, or speak again and most likely would never know who they were.

It had begun the early Tuesday morning of February 23, 1993.

Dee had been standing in line at the Dallas/Fort Worth Airport, preparing to leave on a business trip, when she suffered cardiac arrest. A man standing behind her, Bill Rowell, tried to catch her as she fell, but her head hit the floor very hard.

She was unconscious, and Bill thought the blow had knocked her out. But when he could not detect a pulse or heartbeat, he yelled for help. A nurse standing nearby responded. She immediately began CPR, working for about ten minutes until some paramedics arrived. They performed CPR for another twenty to twenty-five minutes, but for the entire thirty-five minutes her heart failed to respond.

Bill and his wife, Sherri, overheard one paramedic say to another, "Shall we put her in the body bag here in front of everyone or wait until we move her to the ambulance?"

Fortunately, the other paramedic replied, "No. Let's try CPR one more time," and with that final attempt her heart began to beat again.

Dee does not remember going to the airport, collapsing, riding in the ambulance to the hospital, or anything that happened for the next ten days. Sherri Rowell told her everything: that she had prayed for Dee the whole time, and when bystanders had asked how they could help, she told them to "pray like you've never prayed before." And many did.

At the hospital a cardiologist and neurologist evaluated her condition. They were sure that her swollen brain had a blood clot and that she had lost her eyesight. They also believed her hearing had become impaired and her brain had been damaged—it was just a matter of finding out how extensively.

To their astonishment, however, Dee came out of the coma in six hours. Her family was overjoyed. One doctor told her husband that a power far higher and greater than he was had been responsible for bringing her out of the coma. At a second hospital, where more sophisticated and extensive tests were run to determine her condition, the doctors agreed the entire incident was a miracle.

While still not conscious of what was going on around her, Dee had a beautiful experience with Christ. She remembers it was like walking through a totally black void. It was not like a dream—she was rational and knew who she was—she just did not know where she was or how she got there.

Great fear overwhelmed her, and she called out to Jesus for

His help. Then she heard Him speak to her in a voice "more beautiful than anything I could have imagined." He said, "No, it's not time yet." Her husband, Jack, told her he heard her say, "Jesus said it isn't time yet."

When Dee finally awakened, her eyesight and hearing were normal, the blood clot and brain damage were gone, and she knew who she was as well as who everyone else was.

Dee had wanted for a long time to be able to do something special for the Lord. She felt she was doing nothing. Not so now. Since this experience she has had many opportunities to tell about the miracle God performed. She and her husband keep telling people, "The Lord really answers prayer."

Their "Miracle Baby"

At the age of thirteen, Carol had accepted Christ but had drifted away from Him during her college years. Her husband, Dr. M. Bala Subrahmanyam, had grown up in India in a Hindu home. Although he did not actively practice Hinduism, he basically believed it was the best religion.

Ever since Carol had been a little girl playing with dolls, she had known she wanted to get married and have children. But years began to pass after she married in 1975, and no baby had come to bless their home.

Through the years a number of Christians had befriended them and began praying for them. In April 1978, after searching earnestly for truth, they both committed their lives to Christ.

They still longed for a child, but their hopes grew dimmer. They endured many infertility tests, many medical treatments, and much frustration. People in a number of states were praying for them. However, the years continued to roll by with no success.

Finally, in response to prayer, their hopes became reality. In January 1992 the church they attended had a special week of prayer, and the couple made prayer for a child a top priority. The very next week Carol conceived, and in October, Susan Rebekah came to delight their home in Southampton, Pennsylvania. When people express surprise that they have had their first child after eighteen years of married life, they reply that the little girl is their miracle baby.

Two Thousand Witness a Miracle

The March 1948 issue of the *C. A. Herald* reported the miraculous healing of a soldier, James P. Sturgeon, a native of Oklahoma. He was called to service in the United States Army on January 29, 1942, and then from the reception center at Fort Sill, Oklahoma, was assigned to Camp Wallace, Texas, for basic training and then Fort Bliss, near El Paso.

About three weeks after arriving at Fort Bliss, Sturgeon began a hike with a full field pack up Mt. Franklin with the other men. Suddenly overcome by the intense heat, he fell backwards about six or seven feet and lay there unconscious from sunstroke and the fall. The accident caused a skull fracture—"seven different ways"—and left him in a coma for two and a half weeks.

After coming out of the coma, James suffered four paralytic strokes. Each one, he thought, would bring death. After the fourth stroke James lost his voice and needed to have oxygen pumped through a tube into his lungs so he could breathe. An El Paso pastor prayed for him, and God healed his throat, but his entire right side was paralyzed and was gradually dwindling away.

After James had spent nearly five months in the hospital, a number of doctors reviewed his case and decided they could do nothing more for him except send him home. So he received an honorable discharge on August 12, 1942.

In October, Sturgeon went to the annual Oklahoma District Council of the Assemblies of God convening at Seminole. He was in a pitiful condition. He had no use of his entire right side and had to drag his foot around using a single crutch. His head hurt constantly with almost unbearable pain. His eyesight was deteriorating rapidly.

The crowd of two thousand or more in that service would never forget what they witnessed the evening of October 7. James Sturgeon was brought to the platform and seated, with his crutch placed beneath the piano. After the song service he asked to be prayed for. Two ministers anointed him and began to pray, joined by others who gathered around.

"Suddenly," James reports, "like a bolt of lightning the power of God hit me, and I was completely healed." His right hand, which had become withered, straightened out, and he raised his whole right arm, which had been paralyzed.

Sturgeon leaped from his chair like a flash and began jumping around the platform for sheer joy. He was completely healed. No longer would he need a crutch. The huge crowd stood to their feet and for twenty minutes praised God for the miracle they had witnessed.

The owner of the Worth Hotel, where James had been staying, was so impressed that he paid for James's long-distance phone call to Eagle City so he could tell his parents about the marvelous healing. The local newspaper headlined the miracle on its front page the next day, and the whole town was stirred.

James notified the Army doctors of his healing and was told to report for examination on December 10 at the Veterans Hospital in Wichita, Kansas. The doctors could hardly believe he was the same person who had been dismissed four months earlier. Seven doctors, each spending one day, gave him a thorough examination.

Afterwards, an officer told James of their report. There was no sign of the cracks in his skull, and his side, which had withered away several degrees, now had a normal measurement.

When the officer asked James the cause of the change, he testified it was the power of God. The officer replied, "The Big Boy has to come down once in a while to show He is still up there." Though his description was inadequate and ill informed, it is true our wonderful God often reveals His power in miraculous ways.

The Sturgeons, now retired, pastored in Oklahoma and also assisted in missionary work in Germany and evangelized on the boardwalk in New Jersey. James's experience is a testimony to God's love, grace, and power.

Water from a Dry Well

The sponsors of a retreat for the youth of First Assembly of God, Collinsville, Illinois, faced a serious predicament. It was the summer of 1976, and the young people had gathered at the Jerry Anderson home out in the country, with Gary Palermo as special speaker, and God was blessing them as they reached out to Him.

Then, youth pastor Earl Wetter reported, a problem arose. The well ran dry. There had been concern about this possibility because it had been a dry summer and having forty young people use the water might cause difficulty. Neighbors were already having trouble with their wells.

At 1:00 A.M. on Sunday, air bubbles in the waterline indicated the well had run dry. Jerry put up signs asking that no one use the facilities. The leaders hoped the well would fill up during the night.

Their hope was short lived. At six-thirty in the morning, Jerry discovered the pump was still sucking air. He found that the thirty-two-foot well contained only five inches of water. The pipe opening was six inches from the bottom of the well.

The leaders gathered the group, and Jerry explained the situation. He added that he believed God wanted to prove His faithfulness and read from John 14:13–14, "Whatsoever ye shall ask in my name, that will I do, that the Father may be glorified in the Son. If ye shall ask anything in my name, I will do it."

He also read John 15:7, "If ye abide in me, and my words abide in you, ye shall ask what ye will, and it shall be done unto you."

Closing his Bible, Jerry said, "These words are for us today, and we are going to ask the Lord to give us water, not only enough for the day's needs, but beyond today."

The group joined hands and prayed, first asking and then thanking the Lord for what He would do. They checked and found the pump was still sucking only air.

Not discouraged, Jerry asked God to answer their prayer and quoted the Scripture passages. Immediately water began flowing from the pump. They used the facilities with no further shortage the rest of the time they were there.

As the group was preparing to leave, Jerry Anderson measured the amount of water in the well. It still measured only five inches!

The Andersons continued to use water from the well after their visitors had left.

Section Three

Xenoglossolalia

*Each one heard them speaking in his own
language.—Acts 2:6*

Speaking in other tongues was a distinctive feature of the outpouring of the Holy Spirit on the Day of Pentecost. "All of them were filled with the Holy Spirit and began to speak in other tongues as the Spirit enabled them" (Acts 2:4). It was this that captured the attention of the multitude that had gathered. On subsequent occasions when the Book of Acts tells what occurred when people were baptized in the Holy Spirit, Luke records that the recipients experienced the same phenomenon.

The Book of Acts records three major instances of xenoglossolalia (speaking in a known foreign language).

One hundred and twenty believers were baptized in the Holy Spirit on the Day of Pentecost (2:1–18). The bystanders who were drawn to the site heard more than a dozen different languages. The people were not preaching (Peter did that later). They were praising and worshiping God.

On a later occasion Peter, guided by the Spirit, opened the door of salvation to the Gentiles at Cornelius's house (Acts 10:34–48). The Holy Spirit interrupted the apostle's sermon by coming upon the listeners. "They heard them speak with tongues, and magnify God" (v. 46). Later, reporting the event to believers at Jerusalem, Peter said, "The Holy Spirit fell on them, as on us at the beginning" (11:15).

A similar happening occurred at Ephesus (19:1–6). Paul met some disciples who evidently were deficient in their spiritual experience. When he prayed for them, "The Holy Ghost came on them; and they spake with tongues, and prophesied" (v. 6).

Until the Pentecostal revival at the beginning of the twentieth century, nearly all church theologians declared that this experience had ceased after the first century. In fact, it was not welcomed by the established churches. They considered it the result of overworked emotions. Some even attributed it to satanic power.

In recent decades a change of viewpoint has come about in the church world. Large numbers of people from the ranks of the Roman Catholics, Lutherans, Episcopalians, Baptists, and other groups have received the baptism in the Holy Spirit with the initial sign of speaking with other tongues.

I have included in *Acts Today* a number of outstanding illustrations of this phenomenon.

A Two-Way Prayer

In the summer of 1952 at a camp meeting on the beautiful Lake of the Ozarks in Missouri, Grace Carroll remained to pray at the close of the morning service, ignoring the summons of the dinner bell. She felt especially burdened for members of her family in Houston, Texas. She began to intercede in other tongues— little knowing just how far her prayers were reaching.

After the burden lifted, Grace noticed a small, dark-haired woman kneeling beside her, tears pouring down her cheeks, and the woman tried to say something in broken English.

"Are you wanting me to pray for your family?" Grace asked. But the woman replied, "You don't understand. You were praying for my family—in the Croatian language [one of the languages of what was Yugoslavia at that time]. You called names and villages that I know well. You were praying for the sick and the dying, those in hospitals, and so on." She went on to say that she had often heard Pentecostal people around altars praying in other tongues for Yugoslavia.

This is one answer to those who question the value of glossolalia (speaking or praying in other tongues). Here was a Pentecostal who thought she was praying for her own family, but her prayer in the Spirit was also spanning the ocean, and she was interceding for people and places she had never heard of before. (Grace Carroll was for many years secretary to Ralph Riggs, a former general superintendent of the Assemblies of God.)

The Messiah Speaks Hebrew

Those present at that women's luncheon in 1964 would never

forget what happened. They were members of the Women's Auxiliary of the Pentecostal Fellowship of North America, which was meeting in Springfield, Missouri.

Present was Mrs. J. R. (Alice Reynolds) Flower, associated with the Pentecostal Movement since the early 1900s. She was well known for her writings and the touch of God upon her life. Also present was Mrs. J. W. Kofsman, who with her husband had lived and ministered in Jerusalem for many years.

Inspired by the Holy Spirit, Mrs. Flower gave an utterance in another language. Mrs. Kofsman snapped to attention. She knew the Hebrew language well, and the message was in the modern Hebrew language.

"I am the Messiah," Mrs. Flower said in a language she did not know.

Continuing, she exhorted the women to be busy laboring for Christ, for the night was coming when they would not have the opportunity.

When Mrs. Flower began the English interpretation, Mrs. Kofsman, the only one there who understood Hebrew, wondered if the message would match the one given by the Spirit. At first she was disappointed, for it was not the same. Then an abrupt change came in the tonal quality of the speaker's voice, and she began to speak as though she were praying. According to Mrs. Kofsman, from that point on Alice Flower gave in English a correct interpretation of what she had said in Hebrew.

Mrs. Flower, now deceased, was well known for her writing ministry, with many poems, articles, and books to her credit. Her husband, the late J. R. Flower, was one of the founders of the Assemblies of God in April 1914 at Hot Springs, Arkansas. He served for many years as general secretary of the Assemblies of God. Later, their son Joseph filled the same post until his retirement in 1993.

Note: The manifestation of the Spirit called "interpretation" is usually not a word-for-word translation. Rather, it gives, in the interpreter's own words, the sense of what has been said in other tongues. Understanding this explains why sometimes there is a difference in length between the two, or why an interpretation may not correspond precisely to the language it was given in.

A Paraguayan Speaks Korean

Few are aware of it, but in the late '70s many Korean businesspeople began to emigrate with their families to Paraguay, South America, largely because of the international electronics market. To minister to them, Christian churches in Korea began to send missionaries. As a result, several Korean churches now flourish in the heart of South America.

Some young people from these churches have begun to train for the ministry in Paraguayan Assemblies of God Bible schools (one of which is in Asunción, the capital city). However, sometimes it is hard for these students because the textbooks as well as the teaching are in Spanish.

At one point God did something special to encourage the Korean segment of the student body (about 30 percent are Paraguayan). In chapel during a time of prayer, the Korean young men heard a female voice praising God in their native language. They looked around expecting to learn which Korean girl had come in. They saw none.

Then they realized it was a Paraguayan girl who was praising the Lord so clearly in their language, a language she had never studied and of which she knew not a single word. This was an encouraging experience, no doubt; after all, the Holy Spirit is the Comforter, the One who encourages.

A Leader and a Layman Cooperate

Cloyd McCleery of Alton, Illinois, was a man utterly devoted to God. According to a former pastor, Owen Carr, he was much beloved by the young people of the junior high school where he served as a custodian. Because of his warmheartedness, when they were sick or had problems they found it easy to come to him and ask for prayer. Even the principal of the school had benefited from his prayers on occasion.

Unlettered but with a simple trust in God, he was used by the Lord in a remarkable demonstration of Holy Spirit-inspired xenoglossolalia in February 1960.

A statewide ministers institute was in session at nearby Granite City, Illinois. During the evening service, to which laymen had been invited, there was a time when the congregation had begun worshiping God. Afterward, the congregation heard McCleery begin speaking in a language unknown to him. He spoke for some time.

The Scriptures advise believers to pray for the interpretation, also inspired by the Spirit (see 1 Corinthians 14:13). This time it was Thomas F. Zimmerman, newly elected general superintendent of the Assemblies of God, whom the Holy Spirit chose to bring the interpretation. He rose to his feet and stated in English the meaning of the utterance McCleery had given.

In the audience that night was a little woman who, her son stated, "was thrilled to hear and understand the layman as he spoke." Anna Richards Scoble had spent many years as a missionary in South Africa. She had done so after a remarkable healing of damaged vertebrae that increased her height by two and three-quarter inches.

Obtaining permission to speak, Mrs. Scoble told the amazed congregation of the miracle they had just witnessed. Cloyd McCleery had spoken in the language of a South African tribe, Shangaan.

Especially remarkable, Mrs. Scoble said, was the fact that this language is very hard to speak, containing sounds almost impossible to duplicate unless a person has been born into and has grown up in the tribe. McCleery, she said, had spoken the language perfectly.

The message from the Holy Spirit emphasized the famous revival text 2 Chronicles 7:14, "If my people, which are called by my name, shall humble themselves . . . ," and urged the people to look to God for revival. And T. F. Zimmerman had conveyed this thought in the interpretation he gave.

It is reported that as a result of this incident, the host church began a twenty-four-hours-a-day prayer chain that lasted for over three months, bringing great blessing to the congregation.

Both Cloyd McCleery and Thomas F. Zimmerman are now with the Lord, but their Spirit-inspired cooperation remains to testify that God uses anyone, regardless of status, who will yield to the move of His Holy Spirit.

Deaf-Mute Receives Baptism

W. W. Simpson was a veteran missionary who labored many years ago on the Tibetan border in China. In the 1940s the *Pentecostal Evangel* printed his personal testimony of what God did for a man who seemed beyond hope.

Simpson and his sixteen-year-old son, William, had just returned to the Kansu-Tibetan border, and a Pastor Chow asked them to conduct some meetings for the church that met in his house. Attending were eighty to one hundred men, women, and children with a wide variety of backgrounds: Chinese, Tibetan, and those of mixed descent, some believers and some idolaters.

Simpson reported, "In the congregation was a half-breed deaf-mute. He could neither hear nor speak. No one had ever tried to teach him anything (sign language was entirely unknown in that remote part of the world).

"As I looked over the audience and saw his face so destitute of the least sign of intelligence, I thought, *How hopeless he is! How helpless I am to give him the slightest idea of God's grace and salvation.*"

However, the man attended each of the three meetings every day for the entire week. He could hear nothing, but he watched and saw the agony on the faces of the people as they became convicted of sin. He saw tears streaming down their faces as they repented. Then he saw the inexpressible joy as Christ came into their lives.

Toward the end of the week the deaf-mute surprised the missionary by coming to the altar with the other people. Simpson still thought of him as a hopeless case. Surely he had not understood enough of the gospel to be saved.

But Simpson's son, William, full of the Spirit and faith, went and knelt beside the man and laid hands on him in the name of the Lord. Soon the man's body began to tremble, and he wept before the Lord the confession he could not speak. Then the peace and joy of the Lord filled him with laughter.

That was not all! In a few minutes the entire congregation was amazed that God had poured out on the deaf-mute the gift of the Holy Spirit, for they heard him speak with a distinct tongue and magnify God.

Another miracle occurred. After he had spoken in another tongue for a few minutes, suddenly the deaf-mute began to interpret in the Chinese language, expressing adoration, worship, and praise such as only the Holy Spirit can inspire.

W. W. Simpson and the other believers thought God had healed the man's dumbness, but when he had finished, his face beaming with joy, he was unable to speak a single word of testimony or praise. However, many times after that, in prayer and worship, the Holy Spirit spoke through him in tongues and interpretation.

Translating "Jesus"

A problem had arisen in Northern Ghana about the proper way to translate the name "Jesus" into the Dagbani language. The Bible Society wanted the missionaries to refrain from using the name "Yisa" because the Muslims used that name for the "son of Mary" who was a prophet, but not the Son of God. On the other hand, the African Christians did not want to start using the English name "Jesus." They loved the name "Yisa" and knew it meant the One whom they knew to be the Son of God, their Lord and Savior.

Missionary W. Franklin McCorkle reported that the problem was solved by something that happened thousands of miles away.

He had spent most of his time since 1952 with the Dagomba tribe, whose language is Dagbani. He taught in the Bible school where, until 1968, the students were taught in that language.

The missionary had demonstrated his expertise in the language in other ways as well. He had translated into Dagbani the Books of Daniel and Revelation, various songs, Bible school lessons, and similar material. He did all his village preaching in the Dagbani language and needed no interpreter to repeat it in the vernacular of the village people. They would say to interpreters, "You don't have to repeat his words, for we understand what the white man says. He speaks our language like one of us."

In January 1958 missionary McCorkle and his wife were attending revival services at Trinity Tabernacle in Baytown, Texas, pastored by Rev. W. S. Graham. One night, while kneeling in prayer by the front row seats, McCorkle suddenly heard a familiar language—Dagbani.

Turning, he saw a young woman of the church, Shirley Young (who became Mrs. Stanley Holzaepfel), standing with her hands raised, her eyes closed, and saying, "Yisa Masia, Yisa Masia, Oh N Yisa Masia, Yisa, Yisa," meaning "Jesus Christ, Jesus Christ. Oh, my Jesus Christ, Jesus, Jesus," and other praises to the Lord in Dagbani.

According to McCorkle, not only were the words clear and distinct, but the intonation was of a kind that showed devotion and worship. The young woman continued for several minutes worshiping the Lord and calling Jesus the Son of God, "Naawun' Bia."

The next day, Franklin McCorkle wrote his fellow missionary H. S. Lehman in Ghana, who was also doing translation work, and told him, "If 'Yisa' is good enough for the Holy Spirit to use, let us continue using it in our Dagbani language work." And this has been done. An interesting result: This story appeared in *Spoken by the Spirit*. Franklin McCorkle loaned the book to a well-known Baptist pastor who had become interested in the baptism in the Holy Spirit but was not fully persuaded about the reality of glossolalia. This incident persuaded him of its reality; consequently, he rented a hotel room for several days to pray, and received the fullness of the Spirit.

Thanks for a Good Bargain

The Teso language, spoken in Uganda, developed before money was in use in the culture of the people who spoke it. So bartering was the usual method for making an exchange of any kind. After the parties would complete their bargaining—for example, some grain for some tea leaves—the ones involved would say *exalama,* meaning, "Thank you for what you do." Since bartering goes on every day, and each transaction may take hours to complete, the term *exalama* is heard constantly from house to house and village to village.

A missionary priest, Father Albers—originally from Holland and now retired and living in Sault Saint Marie, Ontario, Canada—was well acquainted with this word. For ten years he had lived and taught in Uganda, using the vernacular, and was in constant contact with the native culture and language.

In 1973 the charismatic magazine *New Covenant* reported that the priest for the first time, at a prayer meeting in London, Ontario, heard some charismatics singing in other tongues. He said later, "This occasion stays with me as a God-given evidence and witness for me—weak in believing, slow in accepting, long in doubting."

But that was not all that convinced him this work of the Holy Spirit was genuine. To his amazement the priest witnessed something even more remarkable. He reported, "A woman of mature youth, arms raised and evidently moved, said again and again, *'Exalama.'*

"As it is repeated so often in Uganda, so she repeated it again and again until I was so curious that I interrupted her and asked, 'Have you been to Soroti? Do you speak Teso? Do you know

114

what you are saying?' No, she did not; she had not been there; she had no idea what it meant."

"Thank you for what you do." Every believer should say *exalama* when he realizes what a good bargain he has found in the gospel. It costs us nothing because Jesus paid the price, but oh, how much the Lord lavishes on His children!

Glorious Monotony

Phil O'Mara was becoming very tired, that summer in 1972, of hearing the same phrase in other tongues over and over. He and Steve Peterson, a young American of Swedish descent, were staying in the same home in the Word of God community in Ann Arbor, Michigan.

They had morning and evening prayers together, and it seemed that whenever Steve prayed in other tongues he began with the same words. It was the same inflection, the same accented syllables—everything was always the same! Secretly, O'Mara thought it was very monotonous. He had heard the phrase so often, he knew it by heart.

O'Mara had been concentrating on studying modern African literature, but he was also doing some background reading in the older traditional literature of Africa.

One evening he was reading an article in a scholarly journal on the technique of public recitation. It included some examples from African literature, transliterated into English, with rhythmic markings.

Then he saw it! The identical phrase Steve Peterson had been using each time he began praying in the Spirit: U sishay 'aka-sishayek(i).

Phil O'Mara discovered that this particular phrase is the opening of an epic poem written in praise of Shaka, a great Zulu king, the unifier of his nation in the early nineteenth century.

As O'Mara sat there he carefully checked his memory on the phrase he had heard Steve Peterson pray so often in other tongues. There was no mistake: The phrase on the page and the phrase he had been hearing were identical, accents and all.

Then he looked up the translation of the phrase. He found that it means: "He who can strike a blow, but whom no man can attack." (David Rycroft, "Melodic Features in Zulu Eulogistic Recitation," *African Language Studies* 1 [1960]: 66).

What an apt description of Christ, the King of kings and Lord of lords! And what a beautiful way to begin a prayer!

"He Is Going to Fill You"

At the Maranatha Park Campground, Green Lane, Pennsylvania, there was a large prayer room behind the platform where people could gather after a service. One night in the late 1940s, evangelist A. N. Trotter was encouraging people in the prayer room by praying and praising God with them.

He noticed a group of five or six people praying together. They appeared to be of foreign origin. One woman especially was praying with great intensity.

Sensing that she was close to being filled with the Holy Spirit, Trotter began praying with her—in other tongues—though, he reported, he felt no special anointing upon himself. After about ten or fifteen minutes, the woman was baptized in the Spirit.

After some time and after the Spirit's presence had lifted from the woman to some extent, she arose, and the small group gathered around the evangelist to thank him.

"You helped me so much," the woman said.

"I did?" Trotter replied. "How?"

"Oh, you talked to me in my language."

"What is your language?" the minister asked. "What was I saying?"

"Oh," the woman answered, "you said over and over in Ukrainian, 'He died on the cross for you. He shed His blood for you. He will not deny you now. He is going to fill you.'"

And He did!

The Spirit Answered Her Doubts

Norma Champion is the widow of the late Richard Champion, who was editor of the *Pentecostal Evangel*, official voice of the Assemblies of God. For many years she was "Aunt Norma" to thousands of Springfield (Missouri) area children through her TV program, and presently serves in the House of Representatives for the state of Missouri.

However, in the early 1950s when she was a student at Central

Bible College in Springfield, before her marriage, she had begun to have doubts about her Pentecostal experience. Was it all just an emotional reaction to the presence of God?

As she sat behind a fellow student, Val Keller, in chapel one morning, Norma was again wondering about her experience and the validity of glossolalia. Suddenly she sat bolt upright. Val was speaking quietly in another language, praying and praising God in French.

Norma had been studying the language and was able to understand the message. Val was speaking the language perfectly, experiencing no difficulty with the nasal and throat tones that usually cause a problem for English-speaking people.

When Norma asked Val Keller about it later, she replied she had never studied French and had not even been aware that she had been speaking it.

That settled the question for Norma.

The Showers Were Falling

It was 1943, and O. L. Harrup, pastor of the Assembly of God in Petersburg, Virginia, had noticed a gentleman who had been attending the services on Sunday evening. Of foreign extraction and always quiet and reverent, he would sit toward the rear of the church until the altar service, then he would move forward to the second row to observe.

One Sunday evening as the pastor was walking back and forth encouraging those waiting on God during the altar service, the stranger attracted his attention. Excitedly he was waving his hands trying to get the pastor to come to him.

When Pastor Harrup reached him, the visitor began speaking in broken English and pointing to seventeen-year-old Thomas Emery. The youth was standing nearby with upraised hands and praising God in other tongues.

"The young man is speaking my language!" the visitor exclaimed.

"What language is it, and what is he saying?" asked the pastor.

The man replied that Tom, who (it was determined) knew nothing about the language he was praying in, was speaking in Finnish, saying one sentence especially over and over, "The showers of grace are falling." He would then break out in worship to Christ, praising Him for who He is and what He has done.

117

John 3:16 in German

Beginning in the late 1930s and until 1960, Martin Luther Davidson traveled as an evangelist in all parts of the United States. At one point in his ministry, he asked the Lord for a fresh confirmation of the supernatural nature of his charismatic experience.

He was conducting special services in a Fort Worth church pastored by Oscar B. Braune (now deceased) when something unusual happened. Telling about it later, he said, "In the middle of my sermon, I spoke in tongues in a language unknown to me, for about a minute. To my surprise, the Lord did not give me the interpretation. It bothered me the rest of my sermon."

During the altar service, while the evangelist was encouraging those seeking to be baptized in the Holy Spirit, a deacon with the distinctively German name of Hasselmeier said to him, "Brother Davidson, you are German, aren't you?"

The evangelist responded in the negative.

"Well," said the deacon, "you speak German."

Again Davidson said no.

"But you spoke in German tonight," the surprised Hasselmeier exclaimed. "During your sermon tonight you quoted John 3:16 in High German."

Seeing that Pastor Braune (also German) was approaching, the evangelist asked the deacon to say nothing and see what the pastor would say.

"Brother Braune," Davidson asked, "do you know what Brother Hasselmeier has accused me of being?"

"No, but I know you can sure speak German," was the pastor's reply.

"How do you know?" (The deacon was still silent.)

The pastor said, "Tonight, while you were preaching, you spoke in High German and quoted John 3:16 verbatim."

Second Corinthians 13:1 states: "In the mouth of two or three witnesses shall every word be established."

He Heard a Childhood Song

Charles Ramsay, now deceased, was widely known as an artist for Gospel Publishing House in Springfield, Missouri. For many years his cartoons in the *Pentecostal Evangel* and Sunday school quarterlies illustrated each week's lesson.

Shortly after he was baptized in the Holy Spirit (sometime in 1933), Charlie was kneeling in the prayer room of the Minneapolis Gospel Tabernacle. He began to sing in other tongues in a language he did not know.

Kneeling beside Charlie was John Strand, who began to praise the Lord. When both men arose, Strand explained the reason for his happiness.

Ramsay had been singing—in Norwegian—a song John's mother used to sing to him when he was a child. John knew Charlie did not know the Norwegian language and believed God had allowed this to happen so John too would have faith to receive the baptism in the Holy Spirit.

Shortly after, John Strand did receive the Baptism; he went into the ministry and was a successful pastor for many years.

A Professor Translates

In September 1970 William Buechel, with his wife and eleven other people, was visiting the Eternal City, Rome. The tour included a visit to the famous Catacombs, the network of tunnels which lies beneath the city. It is estimated that they stretch for five hundred miles and contain one hundred thousand bodies of Christians who were buried there.

Because Beuchel's group was small it was combined with a group of forty to fifty Jews from America, led by a professor.

While going through the underground passages of the Catacombs, Buechel felt a strange but irresistible impulse to go up to the professor at the end of the tour and speak to him in other tongues.

This impulse in itself was unusual, for although Buechel had been baptized in the Holy Spirit and had often spoken in other tongues since, he had serious doubts about the experience. He was nagged by the idea that possibly he was forming the sounds out of his own mind.

However, Beuchel followed his impulse, went up to the professor, and began speaking in other tongues. He tells in his own words what happened, "I had no sooner started to speak in tongues than I saw his eyes widen perceptibly, and I thought to myself, *This man knows what I am saying.* When I had finished what probably was a sentence or so, I said to him the one word, 'Translate.' And he did! It was something about praise to the Lord, but I cannot recall now exactly what it was; I was so excited."

William Beuchel asked the professor, "What language is it?" and he replied, "It's Aramaic-Hebrew of the third century, neither before nor after."

Beuchel never doubted the validity of glossolalia again!

Editor's Encounters with Xenoglossolalia

Robert Skinner, former editor of *The Pentecostal Testimony*, official publication of the Pentecostal Assemblies of God in Canada, has had numerous experiences with glossolalia. He told of some of them in an article which appeared in *Redemption*, a publication in England.

Kiswahili

When Skinner was a boy of eleven in 1943, his parents had just returned to Canada after eight years in Kenya, where his father had become fluent in Kiswahili.

The father was the missionary speaker at a camp meeting in The Maritimes. People were praying around the altar after the Sunday afternoon service. A young woman was baptized in the Holy Spirit and began to speak in a foreign language totally unknown to her.

Robert Skinner's father began to weep with joy and to translate into English what she was saying. She was praising and magnifying God in perfect Kiswahili.

A glorious postscript: In that service was a young man, Don Feltmate, with some friends. Enrolled in the Baptist Bible Seminary, he had come with his friends to observe these Pentecostals and even to make fun of them.

When Feltmate heard the father's interpretation and saw the glory of God on the face of the young woman, his scorn changed to thirst, and he too was filled with the Holy Spirit. He changed his plans: he transferred to the Pentecostal Bible College in Toronto and entered the ministry. He pastored several large churches in Canada and served as a general officer of their fellowship.

Perfect English

Skinner's father served for a time as principal of a boy's school in Kenya. There was a special move of the Holy Spirit at the school, and one evening about ten o'clock, he went down to the dormitories to see if all the lights were out.

As he walked in the darkness, he suddenly heard someone praying in perfect Oxford English. Following the sound, he found the Maragoli cook, an illiterate man who knew no English, praising God with perfect diction and grammar.

Russian

Robert Skinner's son Gary, missionary to Uganda, was back in Canada speaking for three days of special services at Eastern Pentecostal Bible College in February 1993. During that time there were many glossolalic utterances with the accompanying interpretation, as the Bible recommends.

A male student had a visitor, a young woman from Germany, a convert of only about two weeks. On the way home he asked her how she had enjoyed the service, which he realized was new and probably strange to her.

Her reply surprised him. She had enjoyed it very much, especially when someone had stood up and spoken in Russian, a language known to her. She had been seated some distance away and was not able to hear every word, but someone nearby had given the exact English interpretation. Neither the one speaking nor the one interpreting knew Russian.

Welcomed at the Wailing Wall

Those familiar with the strong religious feelings of Orthodox Jews know their antipathy toward the idea of a Gentile approaching the Wailing Wall (their name for it is the "Western Wall"). It is probably their most sacred shrine. This is especially true on Saturday, their holy day. But in 1973, Pastor Albert Pyle, now in heaven, received a welcome there.

While on a tour of Israel, Pyle determined to visit the Wailing Wall early one morning before breakfast. Hiring an Arab boy to guide him and taking his tape recorder with him, he started out. He had forgotten it was Saturday, the Jewish Sabbath.

As the pastor and his guide approached one of the main

entrances to the Old City, two men and a woman sitting there raised their hands in protest, refusing to let them proceed. At this moment, Pyle felt moved upon by the Holy Spirit and began speaking in other tongues. The three people immediately changed their attitude and allowed him to proceed unhindered.

Had Pastor Pyle spoken their language?

Coming to the esplanade before the Wailing Wall, Pyle and his young guide started toward the shrine. But some Jews approached them and said in broken English, "No, this is Sabbath!" (Fortunately the pastor had turned on his tape recorder to add this experience to the many hours he had already taped. So what followed was recorded.)

Once again moved upon by the Holy Spirit, Albert Pyle began speaking in other tongues. As before at the gate, the attitude of these men changed. They provided him with a yarmulke, the skullcap used by both the Orthodox and the Conservative Jews, particularly when at prayer, and allowed him to proceed all the way to the Wailing Wall.

What follows is the conversation, transcribed from the tape, between the pastor and a friendly Jew near the Wall:

"Did you understand what I was saying?" Pyle asked.

"Yes," the Jew replied, "it was a language."

"What was I saying?" the pastor continued.

"You were praying to God," was the reply.

They continued in conversation for some time in English.

After returning to America, I played the tape for Dr. Stanley M. Horton, then professor at Central Bible College and the Assemblies of God Theological Seminary. He is a Hebrew scholar and at that time had taught for more than twenty-five years at the college. Although he could not recognize all the words of Pastor Pyle's utterance, he identified certain phrases as Hebrew words of praise.

The Jewish people have returned to Israel from nearly one hundred countries of the world, and many know several languages. There was something in Albert Pyle's utterance that day that persuaded the Jews at the Wailing Wall to accept him as one of their own.

"He Will Convict of Sin"

After going as missionaries to Alaska in 1917, Charles and

Florence Personeus had a long and fruitful ministry. In fact, they opened the first Assemblies of God church in the territory in Juneau. They worked a great deal among Native Americans. (There are many different tribes of these people in Alaska, each with its own dialect.)

One evening a man from the Thlingket tribe, centered in the area near Juneau, attended a service. After listening to testimonies from the small band of believers, he stood and said in broken English, "You people can read . . . my people can't read . . . we need preacher . . . we want you—Klukwan [his village]."

Touched by what seemed like the "Macedonian call" the apostle Paul received, a couple of workers offered to assume leadership of the Juneau church so Rev. and Mrs. Personeus could go to Klukwan.

It was difficult for the Personeuses to minister among the Thlingket people since they did not know the language. They had to speak through an interpreter, the uneducated man who had come to them at Juneau. He would come to the Personeus home the day before each service, and Charles would read and explain the meaning of the words he planned to use so their interpreter could understand and interpret the sermon correctly.

(Speaking through an interpreter can be risky, Florence Personeus has said. Once, while trying to explain the 23rd Psalm, an interpreter described it this way, "The Lord is my goat hunter [they have no idea of what a shepherd is]. He knocks me down on the mountain and drags me down to the beach.")

One night during an altar service at Klukwan, God did a remarkable thing for the Personeuses. A woman began to cry and seemingly was in great pain. There was no doctor in the village, so Charles began to pray for her. Soon, moved by the Holy Spirit, he began praying in other tongues.

A Native American woman kneeling at the other end of the bench where Florence was praying became so excited she crawled across the floor on her knees to Florence and said, "He is talking in our language!"

An extraordinary hush came over the people as they listened in amazement, for the Thlingket language is a strange and difficult one. How could this missionary, who up to then had to speak through an interpreter, now speak in their language?

When Florence asked what her husband was saying in his prayer for the woman, the answer came in solemn tones, "He is saying, 'God loves you, but not your bad life. God wants to heal you and take away your pain, but you must repent and ask God to take away your sins.'"

"He will convict of sin," Jesus said about the Holy Spirit, and this is what He was doing. The woman confessed her sin of adultery, which many in the village knew of but which the missionaries had not suspected. The incident put the fear of God in many hearts and made them receptive to the gospel message.

A Dying Exhortation

It was during the Vietnam War in the late 1960s. Master Sergeant John McElhannon knew his friend George was different from most of the other men in his company. Some of the other Marines professed Christianity, but George lived it. John saw in George a man to be respected and admired, and they soon became good friends. To while away the time, John sometimes tried to teach George some of his native Navajo language, but his friend seemed unable to grasp it.

One day the Vietcong attacked their position, and to John's dismay he saw George fall, critically wounded. Rushing over to his injured friend, John encouraged him, "You're going to be all right. Take it easy and save your strength."

But George was not all right. Moments later, he was gone. However, before he died he summoned enough strength to say a few words, "John, you need God."

The sergeant's eyes widened. George's last words, spoken by the power of the Holy Spirit, were in flawless Navajo!

The words haunted John McElhannon. Later, after being wounded in action, he came back to the United States to recuperate. As he lay in the hospital he could not forget the words— "John, you need God."

He determined to find the faith that George knew, but his search seemed in vain. First in San Francisco and then in Fresno, California, he visited various churches but failed to find the truth he was searching for.

Then, just before leaving Fresno, he picked up a phone directory, and in the yellow pages the name Bethel Temple leaped out at him. A phone call to the pastor led him to a Saturday night young people's meeting, and he soon found that these youth knew George's God.

As John McElhannon unburdened his heart, his new friends

explained it was the Holy Spirit who had enabled George to speak to John in the Navajo language, even though he had never learned it.

The young Marine soon put his faith in Jesus Christ. Now George's God was his God too.

Comforted by the Holy Spirit

Jesus referred to the Holy Spirit as "The Comforter," and Yoshiko, a Japanese housewife far from her native land, found that, indeed, that is His ministry.

J. Clifford Murray, who had come to pastor the Assemblies of God church in the small town of Garibaldi, Oregon, early in 1955, was doing house-to-house visitation. A young mother, Yoshiko (Mrs. Alan) Thomas, was willing for her two small children to be enrolled in the cradle roll department. Later, the children were sent to Sunday school when the nursery superintendent called for them.

At the invitation of a worker, the entire family attended a service, and that day the former serviceman Alan Thomas was reclaimed, and his Japanese wife found Christ as Savior.

But it's difficult to move to a new land with its strange language and customs, and the young wife was often tempted to become discouraged and discontented, even though the family attended the church services regularly.

Then God responded specifically to her feelings. Reverend George Davis had been speaking at the church each night one week in June. One night he spoke on the subject of the baptism in the Holy Spirit.

During prayer time after service, inspired by the Holy Spirit, an American woman, Mrs. Stocker, who had no knowledge of the Japanese language, began speaking in other tongues, "Inomata, Inomata—Yoshiko."

Kneeling beside her husband at the altar, Mrs. Thomas grasped her husband's arm tightly. She was hearing her own name, the family name spoken twice and then her given name, "Yoshiko."

Yoshiko listened intently as Mrs. Stocker continued speaking in Japanese through the Holy Spirit, "I have brought you across the waters and over here so you can find Jesus, and happiness is yours if you will believe."

125

"She's talking to me; she's talking to me!" Yoshiko exclaimed. This was the assurance she needed. God was using Mrs. Stocker to convey a personal message, directly from heaven, to comfort and encourage the heart of a young Japanese mother, who was far from her native land and family. Here was her promise of happiness. As she obeyed the admonition, she too received the baptism in the Holy Spirit.

His Latin Convinced His Priest

Young Robert Doyan of Covina, California, had become greatly depressed and was considering suicide, but in the spring of 1963 he heard of services being conducted by evangelist Willard Cantelon and felt strangely impressed to attend. He found Christ as Savior that first night and a month later was baptized in the Holy Spirit.

Robert and his family had been attending the St. Christopher Catholic Church in Covina. He was an altar boy, sang in the choir, and was a soloist. Now he began using his talents at the Assembly of God, singing in the choir and frequently witnessing about Christ.

Then a crisis arose for the young man. He became quite perturbed when his priest, Father Collins, visited him to learn why he had stopped coming to church and to learn more about this experience he had claimed to receive. After all, the priest knew a lot more about the Bible than he did. How could he answer the priest's questions?

However, the Holy Spirit came to Robert's rescue. After all, Jesus had referred to the Spirit as the Paraclete, the "one called alongside to help." As Robert began trying to answer some of the questions the priest had asked him, he began speaking in another language. It poured out of him so freely that for several minutes he was unable to speak in English.

Father Collins hurriedly got up, said, "I'll see you at another time," and left.

Several days later, Robert received a phone call from the priest, asking him to come to his office for a further conversation. The young man went with some trepidation. But this is what the priest said, "I want to talk with you further about your experience. I realize you don't know what you were saying the other day because you have never studied it, but you were speaking in Latin. I was not familiar with some of the words you used and had to look them up to get their complete meaning.

"It was a warning message in which you said the time was short and that I should prepare my own heart before the soon coming of the Lord Jesus Christ. I have been so disturbed since that day that I have been reading my Bible and studying almost night and day. I want you to tell me more about this marvelous experience you have received."

As Robert began to talk further with Father Collins, the priest fell to his knees, praying to God for mercy, was stricken to the floor by the power of God, and received a remarkable infilling of the Holy Spirit.

It was not long before Father Collins was transferred from the church he had been serving and sent as a missionary to Liberia in West Africa.

The Language Jesus Spoke

It happened in June 1971. A number of people in the Grand Haven-Muskegon, Michigan, Roman Catholic prayer community traveled to Ludington for a prayer meeting with members of the St. Simon's Catholic Church, who hoped that out of the meeting a group similar to that of their guests would develop. They did not expect to witness the remarkable event they did.

About forty people were present, including Monsignor Arthur Bukowski, former president of Aquinas College, and Father Eugene Albesteffer, assistant priest at St. Simon's.

Also present was Rev. Richard Lamphear, pastor of the Assemblies of God church in Ludington. He had become acquainted with some Roman Catholics in Ludington and had told them of his own experience of the baptism in the Holy Spirit.

In the early afternoon, Joan McCarthy, from Grand Haven, felt impressed to speak in other tongues. She hesitated because strangers were present, then finally yielded to the impulse she felt had come from the Holy Spirit.

After Joan finished her utterance, Pastor Lamphear (also inspired by the Holy Spirit) gave the interpretation. The message said to the effect that the people of St. Simon's should be united in whatever course they chose and should not divide themselves into groups. They would find strength in their unity and in their love for Christ and one another.

As the meeting concluded, the leader, Bert Ghezzi, asked if there were any questions.

Father Albesteffer addressed Joan McCarthy, "Have you ever studied church languages?"

"No," she replied.

The priest asked Pastor Lamphear the same question and received the same reply.

Then Father Albesteffer said, "I know what speaking in tongues is from my study of Scripture, but this is the first time I have ever witnessed it. Joan, you spoke perfect, fluent Greek-Aramaic, the language believed to have been spoken by Christ. And, Reverend Lamphear, you gave an almost word-for-word translation of what she said."

Note: The manifestation of the Spirit called "interpretation" is usually not a word-for-word translation, as in this case. Rather, it gives, in the interpreter's own words, the sense of what has been said in other tongues.

Praise in Arabic

It was a time of revival at Central Bible College in 1937. This was not a formal, planned series of services but a spontaneous period of waiting upon God, and classes had been suspended.

One suppertime some of the students had gone through the cafeteria line and were sitting at the tables, when God began to move in a special way. As the Spirit of God began to touch young lives, the meal was neglected, and the praise and worship continued in the dining hall, and later in the chapel, until a late hour.

One of the students upon whom God moved in a special way was Paul Schoonmaker—a quiet and reserved student. For some time he had been seeking the baptism in the Holy Spirit.

Then that evening the Holy Spirit took control of Paul, and he began speaking in a language he had never learned. Nearby was Amelia Joseph (later Mrs. Harold Bullock, and now deceased). Excitedly, she told the students gathered around that he was speaking in a language she understood.

Amelia was of Lebanese descent and for seventeen years had

studied Arabic, one of the three official languages of the country of Lebanon. She knew it well.

Now she was hearing Paul Schoonmaker praising God in Urdu, an Arabic dialect. His first words (transliterated) were: "*Ya rubool koona.*" In English this means, "O God of the universe."

This was not merely an emotional experience. Paul was worshiping God the Father. Later, he would demonstrate his surrender to the will of the God he was praising by going to India as a missionary. After a fruitful ministry there, he went to be with the Lord he loved in 1971.

Called by Name

Robert Blumm came a long way. Born in New York City, early in life he became a member of one of the gangs that roamed the streets, seeking to take vengeance on a society they hated. At the age of thirteen he began taking drugs, and by the time he was sixteen he had become an addict. No one seemed to care for him, and the God he knew little about seemed very remote.

Dropping out of school, Bob joined the Army, vaguely hoping to find some meaning to life. He was assigned to combat duty in Vietnam in 1966–67. Here, fortunately, he became acquainted with two young Christian soldiers who led him to a saving knowledge of Jesus Christ in May 1967. That same night he experienced a further demonstration of the power of the gospel as he received immediate deliverance from the drug habit.

Bob Blumm learned God had additional blessings for him in the experience known as the baptism in the Holy Spirit. Three months after his conversion, he was filled with the Spirit and spoke in other tongues as the Spirit gave him utterance. He says, "Now I had a language to speak to God with and the power to preach the message of Christ crucified, risen, and coming again." (Of course, God understands English too.)

Blumm often slipped away when off duty to find a secret place to pray. One night, after treating mass casualties, he left the surgical hospital to take his heavy burden to the Lord. As he sensed the presence of the Holy Spirit around him, he began praying fervently in an unknown tongue.

After praying for some time, Bob felt the burden lift. At the same time he sensed the presence of someone behind him.

Looking around, he saw two Vietnamese civilian workers. For two months they had noticed him as he prayed from time to time.

He had prayed in the Vietnamese language, they told him, and through him the Holy Spirit had addressed them by their names, Moui and Tinh. The Spirit had called on them to receive both salvation and the same gift that they had observed in the life of Robert Blumm.

Both Vietnamese men received Christ as Savior that night.

Section Four

Unusual Experiences

Now Stephen, a man full of God's grace and power,
did great wonders and miraculous signs among the
people.—Acts 6:8

This section includes fascinating incidents about angels, demons, special guidance, and visions.

Angels

The Bible contains many incidents concerning the ministry of angels (for example, see Acts 12:7). Hebrews 1:14 states they are "ministering spirits" whom God sends as His messengers to assist believers. The Book of Acts records a number of instances when angels provided supernatural help.

At Jesus' ascension, two angels told the disciples that "this same Jesus" would return as He went away (Acts 1:11). An angel delivered the apostles from prison (5:19). An angel (8:26) directed Philip where to go. An angel told Cornelius to send for Peter; he even gave the apostle's address (10:1–6). When Peter was imprisoned, an angel set him free (12:1–10). When King Herod failed to give God the glory, an angel brought judgment upon him (12:20–23).

Our verification for stories about angelic visitations must depend on the sources: the people involved. To be candid, the incidents that appear in *Acts Today* cannot be documented in the same way other miraculous events can. Never did the messengers claim to be angels, but their sudden disappearance, and the fact that no one in the vicinity had known about them, lends credence to the belief that angelic ministry occurred. If not, where did the unusual help come from?

Angelic Travel Agent

Missionary-evangelist Melvin Jorgensen faced a difficult situation when his plane arrived in Belgrade, Yugoslavia. He was scheduled to speak at eight-thirty the next morning at Subotica, nearly one hundred miles away, and the pastor of the church was not there to meet him as he had promised.

Furthermore, Jorgensen did not know the language, and he was not feeling well. How was he to find transportation to his destination? He had no currency negotiable in Yugoslavia to buy anything, including a bus ticket. What was he to do?

(He did not know that the pastor from Subotica had already come to the airport and inquired about the evangelist's flight. He had been told it had already arrived and Jorgensen was not on it. So he had decided to return home in order to reach there before dark. He too was in a quandary wondering what to do about the conference beginning the next day.)

Back in Belgrade, the evangelist decided he should at least get on a bus that would take him to the terminal in the city. But he thought, *What shall I do when I reach the terminal? How shall I find my way to Subotica? How shall I know which bus to take? How can I make myself understood?*

As the bus pulled into the terminal Jorgensen's anxiety increased. There seemed to be a thousand people milling about and dozens of buses coming and going. He was sick and lost.

Then a strange thing happened. As Jorgensen stepped off the bus, his attention was drawn to a man who stood there smiling at him. He was not even sure the smile was intended for him, but he smiled back.

The man was average height and appeared no different from the others, but he motioned for Jorgensen to follow him. Jorgensen did so, for after all he had no other plan.

There were many ticket windows in the terminal. Which was the right one? But he followed his guide until he stopped at a window. The man talked to someone at the window, received a ticket, and motioned for Jorgensen to follow him.

Outside was the bus-loading area. Again, which one should the evangelist take? The man motioned for him to wait for his bus at an empty stall. He refused any payment and left.

The ordeal was not over. The ticket showed it was for the bus to Subotica, but as time went on no bus appeared where Jorgensen was standing. Ten, fifteen, twenty minutes passed. Was this the correct location?

Then the evangelist's "travel agent" appeared once more, smiled, and indicated he should continue to wait. At that moment a bus pulled into the parking spot. Jorgensen got on, showed his ticket to the driver, and they were on their way to Subotica to relieve the concern of the pastor and minister at the conference.

Who was that man? Why was he waiting and looking for a complete stranger? How did he know that Melvin Jorgensen needed help? How did he know the evangelist was going to Subotica?

One hesitates to speak dogmatically and claim the helper was an angel, but does anyone have a better explanation?

The Helpful Stranger

Sister Sharma, an elderly, frail widow of a pastor in India, was frantic. What was she to do? Her family had arranged a comfortable train ride for her from New Delhi to her home in Lucknow. A friend had driven her to the station before dawn and helped her find the seat assigned to her. But just as the train was about to start, a man rushed up and claimed her seat. To her dismay, she found she had the correct seat number but the wrong train!

The train was already moving. Fortunately someone thought to pull the emergency chain, stopping the train, and Sister Sharma had to disembark. Now she was left beyond the lights of the station standing between the tracks with her heavy suitcase beside her.

One could hardly blame her for complaining. "Lord, I prayed that You would take me home safely. Why did You allow this to happen to me?"

Suddenly, a man appeared out of the darkness. "Come," he said, "your train is waiting for you."

Sister Sharma was sure the train she was supposed to be on had already left. And she certainly didn't want to entrust herself to a stranger. What might happen to her! "I'll stay here until daylight," she said, "then I'll do something."

Ignoring her protests, the man picked up her suitcase, took hold of her hand, and led her back to the station. She had never walked so quickly, and she noticed the broken stones along the track did not hurt her feet as they had when she was standing.

Soon the bright lights of the New Delhi station came into view.

The stranger helped Sister Sharma off the tracks and onto a platform, then pointed to another platform across more tracks. "Your train is waiting over there," he said. "Get on my back, and I will carry you across."

"No! I can't do that!" Sister Sharma exclaimed. Sitting down on the edge of the platform, she tried to jump down to go to the train by herself. But the man pulled her onto his back and ran toward the train. It was indeed the train to Lucknow and was behind schedule.

Worried that the train might leave without her, Sister Sharma tried to get on the nearest coach, but the friendly stranger rushed her along. "We will go to the coach where you have your reserved seat," he said.

When they reached the correct coach, the man helped the elderly woman aboard and loaded her luggage on the rack. Immediately, the train began to move. When Sister Sharma turned around to thank the helpful stranger, he was gone.

It was a strange experience, Sister Sharma thought. When he first approached her he did not ask why she was standing there. He had not asked which train she needed. He had not even seen her ticket to learn the correct coach and seat. But he had known all these things.

Could it have been anyone but an angel?

An Angelic Look-Alike?

How did this stranger know his name? Burton Pierce (former national secretary for what is now Men's Ministries) was puzzled.

The day had been one of a series of unusual developments, and now this happening was the strangest of all.

On Friday, August 15, 1969, Burt, with his mother and grand-niece, had decided to drive from a town in Upper Michigan to Duluth, Minnesota, about one hundred miles away. They decided to take a scenic route, which bordered Lake Superior, instead of a more direct one.

After stopping for lunch, they continued driving along the Red Cliff Indian Reservation. About two o'clock in the afternoon, after passing a small roadside park and going only a short way, Burt felt strongly impressed to return to the park and stop there. His passengers questioned his decision, but he followed his impulse.

They had just sat down to rest and pray when a man emerged from another part of the park. It was evident he had been crying. Burt tells what happened, "He walked directly to me, and after a few moments said, 'You're Burt, aren't you?'

"We sat down at a picnic table facing each other, and he poured out his heart. Half American Indian, Bill told the tragic story of an auto accident that happened while he was driving in Oregon. His wife and only daughter had died when the car plunged into a canyon. He was so overcome with remorse and loneliness he had planned to take his own life that day.

"The Holy Spirit had led me to this man so I could minister to him.

"I encouraged Bill to look to the Savior who could meet his needs. I quoted God's Word to him. I prayed with him. And Bill opened his heart's door and asked Jesus Christ to come into his troubled life.

"Then I knew why I had felt so strongly that I needed to come to this remote roadside park. But one thing still puzzled me, so I asked Bill, 'How did you know my name?' I thought he might have heard me speak at a men's meeting, or perhaps we had met before.

"He looked at me strangely. 'Why, don't you remember?' he said. 'We were talking this morning down in the lower park.'

"'But, Bill,' I remonstrated, 'I was a long way from here this morning.'

"'No, Burt, it must have been you. It looked just like you—except you had on a different colored sport shirt. And you told me to come to the upper part of the park and wait for you.'

"I assured him it couldn't possibly have been me and told him where I had been that morning.

"Then he looked at me and asked, 'Well, where are you from?'

"'I live in Springfield, Missouri.'

"He immediately replied, 'You told me this morning that you were from Missouri.'"

All of them there became convinced that the person Bill had met that morning must have been an angelic messenger sent to keep Bill from his plans for suicide until Burt could talk with him and lead him to Christ. Bill had been waiting hour after hour for God's human messenger to arrive.

An angelic look-alike? God is unlimited in the methods He uses to accomplish His purposes; for example, the "man" who appeared to Paul in a vision, urging the apostle to "come over into

Macedonia, and help *us*" (Acts 16:9) turned out to be a woman, Lydia.

Manna—Twentieth-Century Style

It was January 1964, and newlyweds John and Bonnie Eller had been at their first pastorate only six weeks. Now they were facing a difficult situation financially. Their small church in northeast Arkansas was not able to support a full-time pastor, and though John had looked for employment at every business in the small town of 1,700, he had found no openings.

That evening Bonnie had served the last of their food supply—pancakes made with water and sweetened with their last teaspoon of sugar.

"This is all we have, John," said Bonnie. "But don't worry, God called us here, and He won't let us down."

However, the young husband was understandably perturbed. He had never faced a situation like this. When he went to bed, he tossed and turned for several hours. Finally, he arose, went to the living room, and turned on the light.

Then he did something he would not normally recommend. Sitting on the couch, he held his Bible in his hands and let it fall open where it would. Instantly his eyes fell on a verse that stated, "God *is* my strength *and* power; and he maketh my way perfect" (2 Samuel 22:33).

That settled the matter for the young pastor. He returned to bed and almost immediately fell asleep.

The next morning, about six o'clock, there was a loud knock at the side door of the little parsonage. Hurriedly putting on his bathrobe, John opened the door.

Standing at the doorstep was a very elderly man holding two large grocery sacks in his arms. He was wearing a faded red flannel shirt and bib overalls. Thin, stooped, and unshaven, he was carrying a walking cane in the crook of his arm.

"Here, preacher," he said in a hoarse and trembling voice, "you may need these."

Reaching out with both arms, John Eller hugged the two heavy sacks together and carried them toward the little mohair couch in the living room. Placing them there, he turned around to thank his benefactor.

He was gone!

Excited, the pastor ran outside and looked up and down the street. The man was not in sight. John ran around the house and over to the church next door, but there was no trace of the man who had spoken to him moments before.

Returning to the house, John found Bonnie smiling with big tears rolling down her cheeks. She had gone into the living room to examine the contents of the sacks. To her amazement, she found everything they normally would buy: two large cans of pineapple juice, sugar, flour, canned vegetables, meat, and even their favorite brand of coffee!

"See," Bonnie exclaimed, "I told you God would take care of us. He even knows what brands we like."

After breakfast Pastor Eller toured the business district, describing the man who had brought the groceries and asking if anyone knew him. All answered in the negative. No such man had been seen in their community.

During the time of their pastorate there, the Ellers often inquired about the man who had brought help to them in their need. They never saw or heard of him again.

The Ellers have never again found themselves in such dire circumstances, but they have remained confident that the Lord who helped them that time would always supply what they need.

"Where Are the Men in White?"

Veteran missionaries Monroe and Betty Grams had driven their one-ton truck around the tight narrow curves in the Andes Mountains of Bolivia at thirteen thousand feet above sea level. Their destination was Puerto Acosta on the shores of Lake Titicaca, the highest navigable lake in the world, bordering Peru. It was their farthest penetration with the gospel.

They had taken with them two Aymara Indian Christians, Pedro and David, to serve as interpreters. They arrived at an opportune time, for the weekly market day was in session at the local plaza. Crowds would gather to barter their products, such as eggs for salt and sugar, and sheep for fruit, bread, colored dyes, potatoes, and witchcraft items.

The gospel team began to sing and preach, but then came an interruption. Felipe Santa Cruz, the alcalde (mayor) for the region, heard the music as he brought his bull down the mountain to sell. "Why have the syndicate men come from La Paz to use their loudspeakers without permission?" he grumbled to himself. "No one has asked me if they can."

He was drunk and very angry, but suddenly his mood changed as he listened and the Holy Spirit touched his heart. Instantly sobered, he said, "We need this message in this area. Come to my home and start a service."

The missionaries were able to give away every tract they had brought and sell every Bible, New Testament, and songbook.

"Leave someone here to teach us," Felipe pleaded, so Pedro and David stayed. They began evangelizing the vast area along Lake Titicaca and down into the Glacier Mountain area.

Then one morning there was trouble! Loud knocking at their door awakened Pedro and David. Exhausted since they had returned late the night before, they opened the door a little and peered out.

Outside was a large group of angry men. They exclaimed, "Where are the men in white? We followed you in the night [undoubtedly to harm them]. We're waiting out here till they leave. Send them out!"

Pedro and David persuaded them that no one else was there; upon hearing that, the crowd dispersed. It seems evident that God had sent angels to protect these young pastors. Now in that area there are large churches, many pastors, Christian families, and a Bible school. Once more a miracle had opened the door for evangelism.

Housework by an Angel

Gladys Triplett scarcely had enough strength to answer the doorbell that morning in 1941 in Newberg, Oregon. Not fully recovered from the birth of their eighth child, she had spent a sleepless night, and although it was only about ten-thirty, she was already exhausted. She felt too weak to tackle the mountain of dirty dishes, the unmade beds, and the huge pile of laundry. Rev. Triplett, her husband, was absent, being the speaker for a revival meeting in another city, and the burden seemed almost too great to bear alone.

When the plainly dressed woman at the door used the word *prayer*, Gladys, in her fatigue, thought she had come to be prayed for; instead, the visitor said, "I did not come for prayer. The

Father has sent me to minister to you, dear child, because of your distress and great need. You called with all your heart, and you asked in faith."

Then, lifting Gladys in her arms, the stranger laid her on the couch and said, "Your Heavenly Father heard your prayer. Sleep now, my child, for He cares for you."

When Gladys awoke refreshed three hours later, she stared in amazement at the change in her house. All the children's belongings had been picked up, and the floors were clean. Her baby, three months old, had been bathed and was asleep.

The dining table, extended to its full length, was spread with her best tablecloth and set with her finest table service. She was especially surprised to see it was set for thirteen people. The stranger explained, "Oh, you will be having guests soon."

Even more astounding was the appearance of the kitchen. The heaps of dirty dishes were gone; there was a freshly baked cake, a large bowl of salad, as well as other prepared food on the counter. Later, the family learned that even the cooking utensils had been washed.

Most surprising of all was what had happened to the laundry. The basket of baby clothes, a full hamper of family laundry, and all the bedding had been washed, dried, ironed, and put away. The guest was just folding up the ironing board.

How could all this have been accomplished? The washing machine could not possibly have put out that many loads in three hours. Further, though there was no dryer and it was raining, the clothes had been dried.

Gladys knew that that much ironing, three basketfuls, would usually have taken her parts of two days, yet the visitor had done it, along with everything else, all that morning. Later, Gladys discovered that every bed had been made and each child's clothing folded and put in the proper drawer.

As the children arrived from school they noticed something unusual about their visitor. Puzzled, some of the younger ones whispered, "Who is she, Mama? She looks kind of different." The mother explained, "This is a wonderful friend God sent to help me today."

As they talked together, Mrs. Triplett tried to learn more about this friendly helper—who would simply tell her, "Just say I am a friend or a child of God who came because of your prayer."

Shortly after the children's return, Rev. Triplett unexpectedly returned. The meetings had been interrupted because of a death in the host church. With him were five others: the pastor, his wife, and another couple and their daughter. When they sat down to eat dinner, there were exactly thirteen people at the table: Gladys and her husband, their six older children, and the five visitors from the other town.

The mysterious visitor had met Rev. Triplett just before the family sat down at the table and then slipped out.

Who was she? No human being could have done so much in so little time, or have known where to put each child's clothing, or have known the exact number of people who would be present for dinner. The family questioned many people, neighbors, friends, even the police. No one could give a clue to her identity. The only explanation the Tripletts could find was Hebrews 1:14, which tells us that angels are "ministering spirits sent to serve those who will inherit salvation."

Demons

The Bible describes demons as emissaries of Satan, performing his nefarious actions against the human race.

Believers do not become demon possessed (how could they when they are indwelt by the Holy Spirit?), but they can be oppressed.

In His earthly ministry, Jesus often dealt with demons, casting them out when they were the cause of afflictions of various kinds. The Book of Acts also records demonic opposition to the work of the apostles. Jesus had told them that in His name they would cast out demons (Mark 16:17), and Acts records some of these victories.

Acts 5:16 reports the healing of people "tormented by evil spirits." At Samaria, demons "came out of many" (8:7).

At Philippi (chapter 16) a demon-possessed woman harassed Paul and Silas until finally Paul commanded the demon to depart.

At Ephesus (chapter 19) men tried to use the name of Jesus as a magical term to cast out demons, but the possessed man leaped upon them, and they fled wounded and naked.

Acts Today recounts present-day victories over demonic power.

Delivered

As Pastor Tom Rutherford approached the home of Sandy

Smith (the name has been changed) in the fall of 1973, he little knew what would come to light during the next five weeks: that the woman he was about to visit was a priestess of a satanic coven, that she was demon possessed, that he was the target of a plot to ridicule Christ, that he would be battling with Satan. His only concern was to witness to her about salvation.

This is a remarkable story of guidance by the Holy Spirit, of escape from death by divine intervention, of a power struggle against satanic forces, and of victory over the evil powers of darkness.

Sandy's brother-in-law had founded a TV cable company at Bedford, Pennsylvania, and she worked as a secretary. She was phoning delinquent customers, one of whom was Linda Haines, a recent convert at the Assembly of God in nearby Pleasantville, pastored by Tom Rutherford. Linda acknowledged that she owed the money but shared her experience with Sandy, saying she could expect her to be honest because she was now a Christian.

Five years earlier, Sandy had joined a satanic coven devoted to satanism and had become its priestess. (Imitating the Lord and His disciples, each coven has thirteen members, one of whom is leader—a priest or priestess.) Their evil rituals include a version of the Lord's Supper designed to mock Christianity. They use a cup filled with human blood and urine—"Better," they say, "than the Christians' observance, because they use only symbolic elements."

This coven had a special rite at Halloween time—the major event of their year. Several weeks earlier they would select a Christian, such as a pastor, and make out a check to him (symbolizing the thirty pieces of silver Judas received for betraying Jesus). However, before presenting the check to the person, they would write profanity, blasphemy, and vulgar language on it.

Then as they presented the check, they would say, "This is what we think of your Jesus." At the next meeting of the coven, they would listen with great delight to the report about how the recipient reacted.

The coven was discussing who would get the check this year, and Sandy, who would present it, remembered Linda and suggested it be given to her pastor close to Halloween. So working through Linda, Sandy arranged for Pastor Rutherford to come to her house. Of course, neither Linda nor he knew the real reason for the invitation. He was thinking only that he might be able to witness to Sandy.

They were sitting in the living room of the wealthy home, and Sandy was about to arrange for another meeting with Rutherford to deliver the check at a time closer to Halloween. Suddenly the pastor was prompted by the Holy Spirit to say, "Sandy, do you know you are demon possessed? Satan is out to destroy you."

Stunned that he knew, Sandy admitted it and asked, "How did you know?"

The pastor replied, "You need to be set free. I'm going to pray for you."

The visit lasted not more than twenty minutes. Sandy was terrified. How did he know of her inward condition? She had never met anyone who evidently knew her so well.

Rutherford asked some key people in his church to join him in prayer and fasting. He arranged to visit Sandy again and took three people with him: Chuck Collins (both a deacon and a state trooper), his wife, Sarah, and Linda Haines.

When Rev. Rutherford began talking to Sandy about the Lord and quoting Scripture, she reacted strangely: She simply left them, went into her bedroom, and locked the door.

The four kneeled down and began praying. Hearing them angered Sandy, who reacted by playing full blast a satanic acid rock group.

Rutherford told Chuck to go to the basement, find the main fuse box, and turn off the electricity. Everything became quiet, and the pastor went to the bedroom door, planning to confront the woman.

He called, "Sandy, we're here to help you."

At that she burst out of the room like a fullback from hell (five feet eight, she weighed over three hundred pounds). Rutherford feared she might try to kill them, but she dashed down the hall, ran out the rear door, and got into her Fleetwood Cadillac with the others in close pursuit.

The pastor tried to get inside the car to talk with her, but she locked the doors and started the car. Linda ran around and positioned herself in front of the car.

Sandy tromped on the accelerator, but the car wouldn't move!

Racing back into the house, Sandy locked the door. It was an impasse. The group went home and prayed even more fervently. Sandy would have to go back to the coven and report her failure to deliver the check. Time was getting short. She kept calling the pastor, sometimes in the middle of the night. He sensed that she was under heavy conviction.

One time she asked, "If I give my heart to Jesus, will Satan kill me?" Suddenly the voice of a man spoke out of her, "Leave her alone!"

He reported the interruption to Sandy, who evidently did not know the demon had spoken.

Halloween occurred on a Wednesday in 1973. The coven had a meeting, and Sandy had to report she still had the check. Pastor Rutherford's congregation sensed the struggle was reaching a climax, and instead of having their usual Wednesday evening service they united in prayer. After the service a number of members went to the pastor's home nearby and continued in prayer.

The prayer at the parsonage had just begun when Sandy phoned. She exclaimed, "I know what you're doing. Please stop praying for me."

Rutherford responded with holy boldness, "We're going to pray harder."

Prayer continued, and about 11:45 P.M. Sandy phoned again. She was ready to capitulate. "This night has been a bummer," she said. "I want to be delivered." She asked to meet with the pastor, and they agreed on 12:15 A.M. at Linda's home.

Wisely, the pastor took Chuck and Sarah Collins with him. When they arrived, Sandy was already there sitting on a couch. Rev. Rutherford sat beside her and began sharing from the Bible, specifically from Deuteronomy 18 and Galatians 5, which show that witchcraft is sinful and will receive the judgment of God.

Sandy said, "I've got to get out of this," and they all kneeled in prayer.

Rev. Rutherford counseled her, "Just say, 'I plead the blood of Jesus.'" She tried but failed. It took her almost thirty minutes to say even the first word. Then, one by one, she spoke the words.

They heard the demon's masculine voice scream, "You can't have her!"

At the moment Sandy finally said the word *blood,* something remarkable happened. The three-hundred-pound woman ascended from her knees into the air, fell backward, and came to rest on her back. She was going through seizures and contortions.

The group laid their hands on her and commanded, "Every demon has to go, in Jesus' name—Amen."

Sandy's body went limp, and she lay completely still, as if she were dead.

The pastor thought, *Oh, Satan has killed her!*

However, soon Sandy sat up, alternately laughing and crying. It was about two o'clock in the morning now. She said, "I haven't laughed or cried for five years"—the entire time she was in satanism. She was completely normal.

They spent the rest of the night hearing her story. She was asked how she felt when she tried to run down Linda with the car and it wouldn't move. She replied, "I knew there was a power that is greater than Satan's."

Sandy had been totally committed to Satan. Now she became fully committed to Christ. Strangely, her parents had not known about her satanism. She won them and others to the Lord. And for several years after that, around Halloween time, she often gave her testimony.

The check was never delivered. The "mail carrier" was!

A Demon Goes, a Church Begins

It was almost midnight, and missionary Harold Kohl was kneeling in prayer before retiring. He was worn out from a long day of pastoring the Colombo Gospel Tabernacle in Sri Lanka (formerly Ceylon). Suddenly there was a heavy banging on the front door of the house. The pastor groaned inwardly. Who could be calling at this hour? What was the emergency?

The young couple at the door had been attending services after hearing his weekly broadcast. Both looked frightened and distressed. "Daddy is very ill," they said, and explained that they had gone to the Buddhist "light man," then to the Roman Catholic priest, and finally to the Methodist minister, but there had been no help.

Knowing of healings at Rev. Kohl's church, the couple had come to him as a last resort, for none of their family was saved.

As Harold Kohl drove his jeep through the darkness, the Holy Spirit revealed to him that this was a case of violent demon possession. He asked the Lord to forgive him for his former agitation and to give him the spiritual power needed to set the man free.

Outside a small house was a large crowd of people holding torches to light the darkness and talking excitedly. As Kohl walked into the living room, he came upon a horrible scene. Three men were holding down another man, who thrashed around on the floor, yelling loudly and cursing. It took all of their strength to keep him from attacking and harming the other people.

Praying for strength, the missionary ordered everyone from the room except the man's wife and the young couple who had brought him there. As many of the people outside as could peered in the open door and windows.

A spiritual struggle followed. The missionary addressed the demon power, "Demons, in the name of Jesus Christ, who is greater than you, come out of the man."

"Who are you?" was the response. "I'm not coming out."

The man began to thrash more violently, trying to get up. Kohl quickly pinned him back down with God-given strength.

Then Harold noticed a juju that had been tied around the victim's neck. He tore it loose and threw it to the doorway, ordering it to be taken and burned. At first it was not done—the people feared the evil powers it represented. But they obeyed when he repeated his command.

Now came the climax of the spiritual struggle. Kohl addressed the demon in the name of Jesus, "Come out of the man, foul spirit!"

The demon responded, "I will not come out. I was invited here. This is now my home, and I will not leave!"

"You will leave!" Kohl said. "In the name of Jesus, leave now!"

Christ showed himself to be the Victor over the forces of hell. With a big heave and a shout the demon left. The man relaxed immediately and opened his eyes, which were now clear. He stood and exclaimed with joy, "I am free! I am free! Jesus has made me free!"

The crowd parted silently to let God's man pass, awed by the power he had used to set their neighbor and friend free. They had fully expected him to drop dead when he touched the juju.

Harold Kohl seized the opportunity to arrange for meetings to be started a few days later in a gospel tent.

The man who had been delivered, as well as his family, was converted, along with other villagers, and a Christian congregation was formed.

Divine Guidance

When telling His disciples that the Holy Spirit would be "another Comforter" like himself (from the Greek *paraclete*, "one called alongside to help"), Jesus added, "He will guide you into all truth" (John 16:13). The Book of Acts reveals how dramatically the Holy Spirit fulfilled that promise (for example, see Acts 11:12).

Some of the manifestations of the Spirit stated in 1 Corinthians 12 show how this was done. Verse 8 refers to the "message of wisdom" and the "message of knowledge." Notice it does not say a *gift* of wisdom or a *gift* of knowledge. These manifestations are special directions given by the Holy Spirit for special moments or occasions.

First Corinthians 12:10 mentions the "distinguishing between spirits." This would be a valuable asset to the believers as they served God in various capacities. Were they encountering opposition from those motivated by the human spirit, or by evil spirits? Was the suggestion motivated by the Holy Spirit?

Acts 2:17 states, "Your sons and daughters will prophesy," indicating that occasionally foretelling the future would occur.

Acts does not always tell how the Holy Spirit guided God's messengers. It might have been by one of those methods already mentioned, or possibly at times He guided them by principles found in the Scriptures. *Acts Today* records times when guidance came through strong impressions.

The following are safe rules to follow in deciding whether to follow a suggestion that comes to one's mind: (1) Ask yourself if the suggested action is, as far as you can ascertain, good in itself; (2) seek to learn whether your motives are correct—determine if it is truly for God's glory and not just for selfish reasons; (3) seek the counsel of godly people; (4) move ahead while asking the Lord to hinder you if it is not His will.

In Acts 5, while dealing with the deceit of Ananias and Sapphira, Peter undoubtedly received knowledge of their deceit from the Holy Spirit.

When Philip came near the chariot of the Ethiopian eunuch, "The Spirit told Philip, 'Go to that chariot and stay near it'" (Acts 8:29).

In Acts 9:15 the Lord told Ananias of the future ministry Saul of Tarsus would have for Him.

In chapter 10, after Peter had seen the vision that prepared him to minister to the Gentiles, the Spirit told him three men had come to seek him, and he should go with them without doubting (10:19–20).

Agabus prophesied concerning a great famine that "would spread over the entire Roman world" (Acts 11:28).

Paul and Barnabas were sent on their first missionary trip not only by the church but by the Holy Spirit (13:1–4).

In announcing the decision to welcome Gentiles as believers, James stated, "It seemed good to the Holy Spirit and to us" (15:28).

When Paul and Silas wanted to go into the Roman province of Asia, they were restrained "by the Holy Spirit" (16:6), and verse 7 states that the Spirit again would not permit them when they wanted to go into Bithynia. Instead, they crossed into Macedonia, the first advance of the gospel into the continent of Europe.

Paul received warning of his coming imprisonment and suffering at Jerusalem (20:22–23).

When reporting the events that followed his conversion, Paul said Jesus, in a vision, told him to leave Jerusalem, and he would have a ministry among the Gentiles (22:17–21).

While in a Jerusalem prison, Paul received assurance he would reach Rome and witness there (23:11).

During the storm at sea on the way to Rome, Paul foretold there would be a loss of the ship but no lives (Acts 27).

In *Acts Today* we have tried to be very careful in selecting items about guidance. A major proof of their accuracy is that the results brought glory to God.

Saved from a Fiery Death

In September 1993, Raul Ortiz, missionary to Venezuela, was leaving Merida on the two-day trip to Caracas to pick up a shipment of supplies from the United States. He stopped at El Vijia to pick up a pastor who agreed to accompany him. They journeyed on to Barquisimeto, where they spent the night. Watching the sunrise the next day as they drove along, they noticed what a beautiful day it was.

Raul became concerned, however, as they drew near the city of La Victoria. The fuel gauge was registering almost empty, and as they drove ahead and found no gas station, he became increasingly worried.

The next sight they saw only added to their concern, for ahead of them they saw a traffic jam with many cars lined up. "This is worse now," Raul said to his friend. There was no way to pass the other cars, so he got in the left lane and waited.

Suddenly Raul saw in the rearview mirror a red flashing light. It was a policeman opening up another lane and signaling drivers to follow him. Raul managed to follow two cars in back of the police car, with a pickup truck behind him.

147

They were moving very slowly, but at least they were making progress. They had driven only about thirty feet when they saw the reason for the congested traffic: to their left a large excavating machine was at work laying cable. But just beyond was a gas station. Just what they needed—God had helped!

As soon as they had passed the machine, Raul swung the car into the gas station and pulled up to the first pump.

The car clock displayed 7:43 A.M., the attendant was walking toward them, and Raul had not yet turned off the ignition.

Suddenly there was a big BOOM that shook them. Startled, Raul looked toward the sound of the explosion. A huge flame was shooting from underneath the excavating machine. The machine itself flew up like a piece of paper, and a torch of fire rose about 150 feet into the air. The excavating machine had severed a twenty-two-inch gas pipe, causing the terrible explosion.

Raul immediately drove to a safe place away from the gas station, fearing it too might blow up. Then, as he looked back, he saw a terrible scene he would never forget. People who had been nearby were panic-stricken and running for their lives.

The police car was nowhere to be seen. The two cars that had been in front of Raul's car and the pickup that had been behind him were engulfed in flames. People trapped in their cars were screaming for help. Soon the stench of burned flesh filled the air. The heat was so intense there was nothing anybody could do.

Standing there and watching the holocaust, Raul shook as he realized that if he had not needed gas for the car, he would have been one of those consumed by the flames. He thought, *Someone, somewhere, was praying for me.* He told the pastor, "We have been born for the third time."

When they reached their hotel at Caracas and turned on the TV, they heard the terrible details: More than seventy people had lost their lives, and more than one hundred were being treated at the hospitals. Bodies had been incinerated; only bones were found in the debris.

Missionaries have often testified about learning that people back home had prayed for them when they were in great danger. Perhaps indeed someone was praying for Raul Ortiz that September day in 1993, perhaps even you.

Divinely Delayed

In the mid-1960s, Delcie Steward was pastoring in Rogers,

Ohio. She had finished her shopping at a bookstore and was about to leave for home. But then a distinct impression came to her mind (from the Holy Spirit, she felt) that she should not leave yet.

Delcie was puzzled. Had she forgotten something? Moving down the aisle looking at book titles, she prayed, *What is it, Lord? Is there someone you want me to speak to? Is there something you want me to do?*

Time went by, but each time she looked at her watch, again came the distinct impression, *Not yet.*

After some time, she felt free to go home—the mysterious suggestion still unexplained. But very soon she learned the reason. Driving through the rain she saw evidences of a strong storm that had passed through a short time before. A large sign lay crumpled on the roadway. Debris littered the roads. The power was out in one area, and at another site flashing red lights warned drivers that power lines had fallen across their path.

The full impact of God's intervention came to Delcie Steward the next day when she heard more details about the course the storm had followed. If she had left the store at the time she originally planned, she would have been directly in the path of the tornado-like storm as it passed through.

She remembered vividly looking at her watch the day before and sensing the Holy Spirit saying (though not in audible tones), *Don't go yet—wait.* She knew God could have protected her in the midst of the storm, but He had chosen to spare her from the ordeal.

Many believers can recall similar times when God spoke to them by bringing definite impressions to their minds.

When God Negotiates

Thomas E. Trask, elected general superintendent of the Assemblies of God in 1993, related one of his experiences as pastor of Brightmoor Tabernacle, Detroit, Michigan.

Prior to his coming, the church had purchased property and had drawn up plans for a new sanctuary to seat twenty-five hundred people. Then city officials became upset over the traffic problems that might occur at that location. There was much debate, and finally the city said no to the proposal.

The situation seemed hopeless, but the congregation engaged

in earnest prayer for God's guidance. Church leaders then learned about a twenty-three-acre tract of land, which was twice the size of the plat the church already owned but could not use.

However, another roadblock arose to hinder progress. The property was owned by the Shriners. When Pastor Trask went to talk with the potentate of the organization about the possibility of acquiring the property, he received little encouragement. They had obtained the site ten years earlier and had paid taxes on it ever since.

The Shriners had surveyed the entire Detroit metropolitan area, and this location, with its freeway accessibility, was the one they had selected. It would be the site for their new temple.

Mr. Kelsner, the potentate, said they had paid $450,000 for the property. Furthermore, he showed the pastor official offers from two other organizations, each for over a million dollars.

Undeterred, Pastor Trask said, "We'd like to make an offer," and the potentate said he was welcome to do so.

When the pastor said, "We'd like to make a bid of $450,000," Kelsner appeared stunned. He was amazed the church would offer so little, but promised to take it to the Shriners' Board for their consideration.

A few days later, Brightmoor Tabernacle received a letter from Potentate Kelsner stating that much to his amazement the board had voted to accept the comparatively small amount.

The secret? The church had simply gone to a "Higher Potentate," and God had done the negotiating. Today, Brightmoor Tabernacle stands as a testimony that God allowed the earlier "no" from the city officials because He had something better in store for His people.

Flight Changed, Life Spared

At 9:00 A.M. Wednesday, December 21, 1988, Grace Mitchell of West Des Moines, Iowa, received the worst news of her entire life.

For some time she had felt a cloud over her. She and her husband, Leo, were expecting their son, Stephen, to come home for Christmas. He was completing two years of study at a college in London, England, and they had not seen him in all that time.

Why Grace was so perturbed she did not know, but she had a strange foreboding. It was the Christmas season, and severe winter weather made air travel dangerous.

She turned to the Lord for help in conquering this fear, and God gave her calm. Part of her prayer was, "Lord, send that same cloud that led the Israelites out of Egypt to the Promised Land." It had been their guide day and night. Stephen also needed divine guidance.

Their son had phoned his parents telling them he would be leaving on a 747 jet at 9:00 A.M. London time and would phone them again when he arrived stateside.

The Mitchells were at the hospital for Leo's annual checkup that Wednesday morning when Grace strolled into a waiting room where a TV was situated. She had been there only a few moments when a news report interrupted the scheduled program. It was a bulletin from London, England. The flight that had left London at 9:00 A.M. London time had been demolished by a terrorist's bomb over Lockerbie, Scotland. It appeared there were no survivors!

Rushing back to the doctor's office, Grace was so overwhelmed she was almost incoherent. As she tugged at her husband's arm, people thought she was having a heart attack. She gestured, "No," and stammered, "Plane . . . London . . . crash . . . all dead . . . news, TV!"

Leo immediately ran to hear the news, then to the nearest phone to ask for confirmation. No further information was available, and officials could only advise them to return home and maintain a vigil by the telephone to receive details as they came in.

Grace said, "I died a slow death from 9:00 o'clock in the morning until 3:30 in the afternoon. Was this to be the final chapter in my son's life?"

At 3:30 P.M. the phone rang. Shaking with anxiety, Leo answered the phone, then yelled, "Grace, it's Stephen!" The mother could scarcely believe the wonderful news. "It can't be," she exclaimed. "Everyone died—there were no survivors."

But it really was Stephen. God had sent that "guiding cloud," and his life had been spared. He told his ecstatic parents that fifteen minutes before the ill-fated flight took off, he had checked with the agent about where the flight would land in the United States. He learned it would land in Detroit, and he would have to wait there for four hours before continuing.

Stephen had asked the agent, "I have friends waiting for me in Chicago to drive me home to Des Moines, Iowa. Do you have any flights going directly to Chicago?"

The agent replied, "Yes! We just happen to have two cancellations on another flight leaving at nine-thirty." (Stephen was traveling with a classmate.)

They chose to change to the other flight! The Holy Spirit, typified by the Old Testament cloud that directed Israel, had guided Stephen.

The joyous mother reported the experience had influenced her son to become a deeply committed Christian.

A Miracle of Circumstances

If it had not been for God's protection and His guidance of a succession of individuals, Vivian Katter would not have survived the accident on July 20, 1951.

A service was in progress during the evangelistic services conducted by Lorne Fox. It was held in a large tent just outside the Minneapolis city limits. The City of Lakes Church, pastored by Vivian's husband, Wilson, was one of the sponsoring churches.

Suddenly a wind began to blow, increasing in intensity. Men unrolled the flaps of the tent to protect the congregation from the wind and the rain that had begun to fall. As the storm worsened, men and boys hurried to hold down the poles.

Their attempts failed when a sudden blast of wind raised the entire tent. There was a sudden pop, and the lights went out. Four of the five central steel poles were taken up with the tent and strewn on the ground. The fifth pole fell over, hitting Vivian Katter on the side of the head, knocking her unconscious as she fell from her seat to the ground.

The next thing Vivian knew, a stranger was helping her over and around scattered chairs and bringing her to a car, which had room for just one more person. (Twenty years later she would meet the man whom God guided to her.) As the driver waited for traffic to clear, Vivian wanted to get out and walk across the open field to the nearby parsonage. Again God guided her. She did not realize how badly injured she was. The field was a peat bog, made worse by the rain, and if she had tried to go across by herself she might well have perished there in the darkness.

Fortunately, Vivian remained in the car and was taken to the parsonage. There her husband realized she needed help and called an ambulance. At the time he did not realize how precious time was—but God knew.

By the time they reached St. Barnabas Hospital in downtown Minneapolis, the patient's left side was paralyzed, and she was unconscious. The first brain surgeon called could not come because a fallen tree blocked his driveway. The second brain surgeon, who operated in seven hospitals in the area, was available and arrived in twelve minutes.

Another interesting facet of God's care for His child: The surgeon had only one set of instruments, and they were at St. Barnabas Hospital already sterilized for a surgery planned for the next morning. So they were immediately available for the emergency surgery. Later Dr. C. Kent Olson told Wilson Katter that if surgery had been delayed fifteen or twenty minutes, Vivian would not have survived.

In addition to the paralysis on the left side, Vivian's right eye was paralyzed. The blow to her head had caused brain hemorrhage, her body had turned purple, and a "death sweat" had come upon her.

Dr. Olson removed some bone from a large indented area in her skull and sewed up the skin. From a medical viewpoint her chances for recovery seemed slim, if not impossible. A letter sent later by the doctor acknowledged the various ways God had worked that night, saying, "We do our best for Him."

God answered the prayers of relatives and other believers, and Vivian fully recovered. Twenty years later, when the Katters were conducting services for a Minneapolis church, a man named Trevor Mingaye introduced himself to Vivian. He said God had impressed him to go to the meeting the night of the storm. He was the one who had found her struggling to her feet and helped her to the car. His response to God's voice had made him one of the numerous instruments God had guided and used that night.

"Every Place . . . Yours"

A minister, who prefers to remain unknown (so we will refer to him as Joe), had an extraordinary faith experience years ago when he was a senior at Central Bible Institute (now College). At that time, each Sunday many squads fanned out from Springfield, Missouri, to hold services in schoolhouses, homes, abandoned churches, and other places. Seniors served as pastor-leaders of the groups.

The squad led by Joe conducted services at a small community church not far from the city. The Lord had laid a heavy burden upon Joe and his squad to reach the people for God. They often met for prayer with this in mind. At a January evening service there was a breakthrough, and two young boys were saved.

Joe was delighted at this initial answer to prayer, and as he rose from prayer he felt impressed to claim the promise "Every place where the sole of your foot shall tread shall be yours" (Deuteronomy 11:24).

He determined to carry out his part—literally—and walked up and down the one middle aisle and between each row of seats claiming them for God. He could not go in the second row on the right-hand side from the platform because some people were seated there, so he waited until they moved, then finished the task of claiming all of the small auditorium.

Before going to bed that night he wrote in his diary about what had happened, ending with "Praise the Lord!" and adding a row of exclamation points.

In April Joe and the squad determined to conduct revival services with Joe as the speaker. God honored their faith, and a number of people were saved. It was a wonderful trial run for an embryonic preacher, encouraging his faith to believe God for an effective ministry. The most interesting feature of the meetings was that no one was saved at the altar but at various places in the small church. And the first ones converted were in that second row, the last one Joe had claimed!

Sometime later, after he had graduated and entered full-time ministry, Joe decided to look in his diary to review what had happened. He saw at the January entry the row of exclamation points and decided to count them. They numbered twelve, the exact number of people who found salvation during the special services!

Joe was reminded of the experience of Elisha and the king of Israel, when the prophet told him to take arrows representing victory over the enemy and strike them on the ground (see 2 Kings 13:14-19). The king struck only three times, not really doing so in faith. Elisha rebuked him saying that he would have only three victories. Joe was glad he had struck with his pen at least twelve times.

Split-Second Timing

Bob Unterseher was listening carefully to the roar of the 875

Versatile four-wheel drive tractor he was operating. It would tell him how deep the bit on the earthmover he was pulling was sinking into the ground; the change in rpm's would guide him. It was imperative that he keep looking straight ahead so the drainage ditch he was building would follow the prescribed course, enabling water to flow properly.

Bob and his wife had resigned the church at Hettinger, North Dakota, two months before and were planning to enter the evangelistic ministry. Jon Liechty had hired him to work for one month; it would ease the present financial strain. So he was determined to do good work on this drainage ditch job.

Suddenly something strange happened. Bob felt a strong compulsion to glance over his left shoulder. The impulse must have come from God at the exact moment of need; otherwise he would not have seen a man falling under the front wheel of the earthmover, and the man would have been crushed to death.

Bob's feet hit the clutch and the brake at the same time. The huge tractor stopped abruptly, and the engine began to race at full throttle.

The man was Wesley Loven, Bob's longtime friend and Jon Liechty's brother-in-law. He was scheduled to retire in a couple of months, and now this tragedy had happened.

What was Bob to do? It was a dangerous situation. The huge wheel was directly on top of the man, pinning him to the ground. Bob reached for the hydraulic lever to lift the bit out of the ground, then pulled his hand back realizing that if he did, all the weight of the dirt in the scraper would press down on Wesley's chest and crush him.

As quickly as possible Bob put the tractor into reverse, at the same time he wondered if it would move with the bit buried deep in the soil. As Bob began to release the clutch, black smoke billowed out of the exhaust pipe, the rpm's dropped, and the tractor began to shudder. It was a delicate maneuver. If the motor died, his friend would not survive.

Bob breathed a sigh of relief, for the jerking motion seemed to loosen the earth's grip on the scraper. The accident victim was free. Bob raced to his side.

Was Wesley Loven alive? Bob wondered. The man's face was white and without expression. Bob had worked for six years as an emergency medical technician, so he knew the situation was critical. Loven had no respiration or pulse, and there was the possibility he was bleeding internally. Bob kneeled beside his friend and cried out, "Spare his life, God! Spare his life!"

As Bob prayed, he heard a faint sound as Wesley began to moan, and his eyes opened slightly. Bob was encouraged. Putting Wesley into a pickup, he rushed him to the hospital thirty miles away. After an hour of X rays, the doctor came to the waiting room and asked Bob to describe in detail what had happened. Afterward he slowly shook his head and said, "There's nothing wrong with him, only a slightly separated pelvis."

God helped all the way, but the start of the miracle was the impulse Bob received from God to turn his head at just the right moment.

Protected During World War II

As World War II began, a few men who attended First Assembly of God in North Little Rock, Arkansas, were drafted into the military. It appeared to the people of the church that the war would not last long, perhaps only a few months, and conditions would get back to normal.

Instead, George Murry reports, the draft began taking a steady stream of men from the church, and soon it had 106 men scattered around the globe serving in every theater of action.

The mothers of the church felt a deep concern for the safety of these men and began to meet each noon to pray very specifically for their needs. They continued their vigil until peace was declared more than three years later.

George Murry reported, "A few men, myself included, were wounded, but not one man lost his life in combat. Each time I look into a mirror and see the scar where a bullet struck my face, I breathe a prayer of thanksgiving for a band of godly mothers who cared enough to spend time in prayer. Their intercession is the reason I am alive to write this."

Visions

Webster's Collegiate Dictionary defines a vision as "something seen in a dream, trance, or ecstasy; especially: a supernatural appearance that conveys a revelation," and such was promised by the Bible (see

Acts 2:17). A vital factor in proving a vision authentic is the personal character of the person involved. The accounts in the Book of Acts present these kinds of persons.

As Stephen, the first martyr, was about to be stoned to death, he "saw the glory of God, and Jesus standing at the right hand of God" (Acts 7:55).

After Saul had been brought blind to Damascus, following his meeting with Jesus on the road, God spoke to the disciple Ananias, telling him that Saul "in a vision . . . [had] seen a man named Ananias come and place his hands on him to restore his sight" (9:12). (Later, in his speech before King Agrippa, Paul referred to the Damascus Road experience as "the heavenly vision" [Acts 26:19].)

An angel appeared to Cornelius, telling him to send for Peter, who would tell him what he should do (10:1–6).

God used a vision of a great sheet containing all kinds of creatures to prepare Peter for believing that Gentiles, as well as Jews, could receive salvation (10:9–15; 11:4–9).

And, as I mentioned before, the Holy Spirit had kept Paul and Silas from fulfilling their plans of "preaching the word in the province of Asia," bringing them to a point of indecision at Troas. There "during the night Paul had a vision" (16:9) of a man of Macedonia pleading with him to come and help them. This led to the gospel's being brought to Europe for the first time.

At Corinth Paul met strong opposition from the Jews, but then "one night the Lord spoke to Paul in a vision," assuring him of His protection (18:9).

In this section of *Acts Today,* you will read of some remarkable visions. They foreshadowed significant advances for the gospel. This, of course, is the major reason for displays of God's supernatural power.

A Modern Macedonian Call

Dean Galyen would never forget that night at a camp meeting in 1964. He had just graduated from high school, where his excellent record had won him a full scholarship to the University of Wisconsin. Being a preacher's kid himself and remembering the persecutions his family had endured because of their Pentecostal faith, he avoided any thought of entering the ministry.

Instead, Dean had decided he would serve God as a dedicated layman. The wealth he expected to acquire would be used to advance the gospel. His scholarship would be the first step in that direction.

In the prayer room after the service, Dean talked to God about his grandiose plans. Later, he realized he had been bragging as though he alone were responsible for his achievements. But God kept on dealing with him, saying, *My plans are not your plans.* Finally, in complete submission, Dean Galyen fell to his knees and prayed, "Not my will but Thine be done."

Suddenly an African man appeared to him in a vision, declaring, "You must go into the ministry for my sake."

So awesome and personal was the experience that Dean told no one about it for eighteen years. At the same time, he responded to God's call and enrolled at North Central Bible College in Minneapolis. Through the years he constantly prayed for the African man who had appeared to him.

In 1972 Rev. Galyen accompanied some members of his St. Louis congregation on a Mobilization and Placement Service construction assignment to Africa's French-speaking Ivory Coast (Côte d'Ivoire). Feeling it was time to break his silence, he told his people about the vision of eighteen years earlier and expressed his conviction that he would see the man during this trip.

Everywhere the team went, Dean Galyen looked for the person in the vision but did not see him. Their major task was to help build a church in the town of Man. Surely he would see him there! But two weeks passed, and he did not appear.

At ten o'clock in the morning, the last day of work in the town, a man walked through the church door. Dean says, "My mouth fell open, and my heart nearly jumped out of my chest." It was the man he had seen in the vision eighteen years before!

Rushing over to missionary Don Corbin, he exclaimed, "Who is that man?"

"That's Elizabeth's father," Don replied. Elizabeth was a member of the church who had helped the team by carrying water from the river for mixing cement.

An interesting (and awkward) conversation followed as Dean and Don met with Elizabeth and her father, Jean Waye. Dean spoke in English, Don translated into French, which Elizabeth translated into her father's tribal dialect.

The eighteen-year-old vision had been fulfilled. As they compared the time of Dean's vision and Jean's conversion, they discovered it had occurred at about the same time—possibly the same night.

For many years Jean and his wife had been the only Christians in their remote jungle village. They had been greatly persecuted, and once Jean had been so severely beaten he was left for dead. They had desperately needed prayer support, and God had provided it for eighteen years.

In 1993 Dean and Peggy Galyen returned to Africa as missionaries.

"Take off Your Glasses"

Could this really be the voice of God? Doris Wood wondered, for it seemed a voice within her was saying, *Doris, take off your glasses.*

Doris, daughter of veteran missionaries George and Elizabeth Wood, had experienced severe vision problems all her life, with only about 50 percent sight in one eye and 20 percent in the other. It was necessary for her to wear very thick glasses.

Now, in late 1951, she was a student at Central Bible Institute (now College) in Springfield, Missouri. A great time of revival had come to the school, and classes were suspended while the faculty and students spent time in prayer and worship. The atmosphere was conducive to faith.

Doris's first impulse when the directive came to her mind was to dismiss it as a false impression. Since she had grown up in the Assemblies of God, prayers for her healing had frequently been offered. However, the poor vision had persisted, and she had given up expecting deliverance.

But the voice came again, *Doris, take off your glasses.*

Again she doubted the idea was genuine, but when the voice came a third time, she argued, "But if I take them off, I don't ever want to put them back on."

At that moment God did something special for Doris. She fell into a trancelike state and began to see a vision of Christ on the cross with blood flowing from His wounds. In her vision she reached up her hand to the blood, took some, and applied it to her eyes.

The young woman was so conscious of the presence of Christ in the vision she was unaware of her physical actions. Taking off her glasses she threw them across the chapel platform.

Doris was instantly healed! However, she remained for a long time in her trancelike state, worshiping the Lord in other tongues. Even after returning to her dormitory room, she was not able to speak, except in an unknown tongue, until the morning.

Her brother, George Wood, general secretary of the Assemblies of God, recalled how beautiful she appeared to him when she returned home for the Christmas vacation.

Doris never wore the glasses again.